GRADES 4–6

Power Practice MATH

100 Engaging Reproducible Activities to Build Basic Skills

Table of Contents

Number and Operations
- Place value of whole numbers 4
- Identifying place value 5
- Comparing and ordering whole numbers 6
- Comparing whole numbers and decimals 7
- Classifying numbers 8
- Properties of integers 9
- Integers on a number line 10
- Ordering integers 11
- Properties of rational numbers 12
- Comparing, ordering rational numbers 13
- Finding squares and square roots 14
- Adding whole numbers 15
- Subtracting whole numbers 16
- Subtracting across zeros 17
- Estimating 18
- Multiplying whole numbers 19
- Multiplying by 3 digits 20
- Dividing whole numbers 21
- Dividing whole numbers with remainders 22
- Dividing with 2-digit divisors 23
- Equivalent fractions, decimals, percentages 24
- Adding like fractions 25
- Adding mixed numbers 26
- Subtracting fractions 27
- Multiplying fractions 28
- Dividing fractions 29
- Adding and subtracting money 30
- Multiplying decimals 31
- Dividing decimals by whole numbers 32

Geometry
- Identifying lines 33
- Identifying angles 34
- Drawing common polygons 35
- Identifying quadrilaterals 36
- Classifying triangles 37
- Identifying geometric solids 38
- Similar and congruent polygons 39

Similar and congruent polygons 40
Identifying symmetry 41
Translations, rotations, and reflections 42
Locating points on a grid 43
Graphing ordered pairs 44
Coordinate graphing 45
Constructing circles 46

Measurement
Using customary measurement 47
Using customary measurement 48
Using metric measurement 49
Understanding metric measurement 50
Understanding customary measurement 51
Understanding Fahrenheit temperature 52
Celsius and Fahrenheit temperature 53
Determining elapsed time 54
Finding area 55
Area of irregular figures 56
Finding perimeter 57
Finding area and perimeter 58
Finding volume 59
Finding circumference 60
Finding area of circles 61

Data Analysis and Probability
Finding probability 62
Using a spinner 63
Using a frequency table 64
Interpreting data 65
Determining the fairness of a game 66
Finding mean, median, mode, and range 67
Reading and interpreting a bar graph 68
Constructing a bar graph 69
Reading, interpreting pictographs 70
Constructing pictographs 71
Reading, interpreting line graphs 72
Constructing line graphs 73
Reading, interpreting circle graphs 74
Constructing circle graphs 75
Reading and interpreting stem-and-leaf plots 76
Constructing stem-and-leaf plots 77
Choosing the appropriate graph 78

Problem Solving
Working backward 79
Working backward 80
Using logic 81
Using logic 82
Using guess and check 83
Using guess and check 84
Making an organized list 85
Making an organized list 86

Making a table 87
Making a table 88
Finding a pattern 89
Finding a pattern 90
Acting it out 91
Acting it out 92
Drawing a picture 93
Drawing a picture 94

Algebra
Understanding algebraic properties 95
Using algebraic expressions 96
Using input/output tables 97
Graphing ordered pairs 98
Finding ordered pairs 99
Understanding inequality symbols 100
Finding addends and factors 101
Writing equations 102
Calculating integers 103

Answer Keys 104–112

Project Manager: Cindy Mondello
Staff Editors: Denine T. Carter, Cayce Guiliano, Peggy W. Hambright, Deborah T. Kalwat, Scott Lyons, Diane F. McGraw
Contributing Writers: Julia Alarie, Marcia Barton, Jan Brennan, Colleen Dabney, Therese Durhman, Ann Fisher, Michael Foster, Terry Healy, Kimberly Minafo, Jennifer Roy, Dana Sanders, Denise Tillery, Karen Turner, Patricia Twohey
Copy Editors: Gina Farago, Karen Brewer Grossman, Karen L. Huffman, Amy Kirtley, Debbie Shoffner
Cover Artist: Nick Greenwood
Art Coordinator: Nick Greenwood
Artists: Teresa R. Davidson, Theresa Lewis Goode, Nick Greenwood, Mary Lester, Clint Moore, Kimberly Richard, Greg D. Rieves, Rebecca Saunders, Barry Slate
Typesetters: Lynette Maxwell, Mark Rainey

President, The Mailbox Book Company™: Joseph C. Bucci
Book Development Managers: Stephen Levy, Elizabeth H. Lindsay, Thad McLaurin, Susan Walker
Book Planning Manager: Chris Poindexter
Curriculum Director: Karen P. Shelton
Traffic Manager: Lisa K. Pitts
Librarian: Dorothy C. McKinney
Editorial and Freelance Management: Karen A. Brudnak
Editorial Training: Irving P. Crump
Editorial Assistants: Terrie Head, Melissa B. Montanez, Hope Rodgers, Jan E. Witcher

www.themailbox.com

©2001 The Education Center, Inc.
All rights reserved.
ISBN #1-56234-471-4

Except as provided for herein, no part of this publication may be reproduced or transmitted in any form or by any means, electronic or mechanical, including photocopying, recording, or storing in any information storage and retrieval system or electronic online bulletin board, without prior written permission from The Education Center, Inc. Permission is given to the original purchaser to reproduce patterns and reproducibles for individual classroom use only and not for resale or distribution. Reproduction for an entire school or school system is prohibited. Please direct written inquiries to The Education Center, Inc., P.O. Box 9753, Greensboro, NC 27429-0753. The Education Center®, *The Mailbox*®, the mailbox/post/grass logo, and The Mailbox Book Company™ are trademarks of The Education Center, Inc., and may be the subject of one or more federal trademark registrations. All other brand or product names are trademarks or registered trademarks of their respective companies.

Manufactured in the United States
10 9 8 7 6 5 4 3 2 1

Name: _____   Power Skill: Place value of whole numbers

Six of One, Half Dozen of Another

Chica Chicken challenges you to use "egg-ceptional" thinking and the place-value clues below to write the missing numbers. **Hint:** Each number contains at least one 6.

1. • The hundreds digit is 6.
   • The ones and tens digits are the same.
   • The ones digit plus the tens digit equals the hundreds digit.

2. • The thousands digit is 6.
   • The tens digit is 1 more than the ones digit.
   • The tens digit is 1 less than the hundreds digit.
   • The sum of the ones, tens, and hundreds digits is equal to the thousands digit.

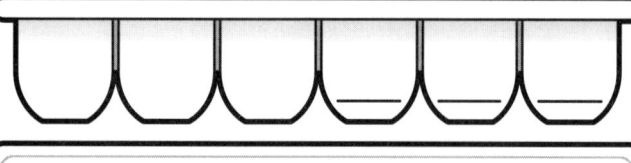

3. • The hundred thousands and the ones digits are the same.
   • The ten thousands and the tens digits are the same and are 1 more than the ones digit.
   • The thousands and hundreds digits are the same and 1 less than the tens digit.
   • The sum of the digits in the thousands and hundreds places equals 12.

4. • The thousands digit is 6.
   • The tens digit is double the ones digit.
   • The hundreds digit is double the tens digit.
   • The ten thousands digit equals the hundreds digit minus the ones digit.
   • The sum of all the digits is 16.

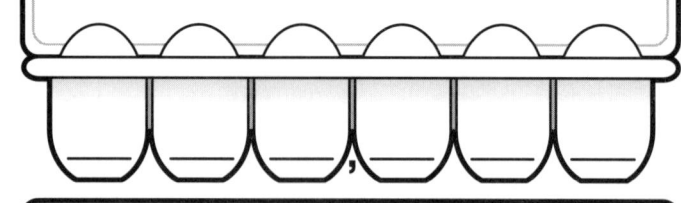

5. • The product of 6 times 6 gives the digits for the tens and ones places.
   • The ones digit is even.
   • The hundreds digit is the sum of the ones and tens digits.

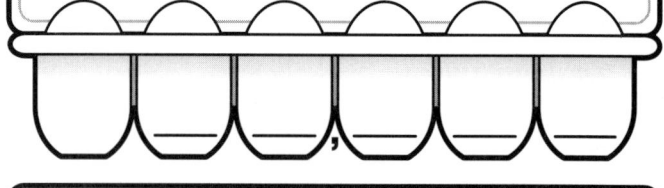

6. • The thousands digit is even and the ones digit is odd.
   • The hundreds digit is the product of the thousands digit and the ones digit.
   • The hundreds digit is the same as the tens digit.
   • The tens digit is 6.

BRAINWORK: On the back of this sheet, write a 4-digit number containing a 6. Then write clues like those above and challenge a friend to find the number.

Name: _____   Power Skill: Identifying place value

Name That Number System

Many different number systems have been used throughout history. In the United States, the base 10 system, containing the symbols 0 to 9, is used. One ancient system used in the past contained symbols such as a tadpole, a coiled rope, and a lotus flower to represent numbers.

Directions: Read each number below. Decide whether the place value listed for the underlined number is correct or incorrect. Then color the corresponding box. After you're done, the unshaded boxes will reveal the people that used a tadpole, a coiled rope, and a lotus flower instead of numbers and what these symbols were called.

Number	Place Value	Correct	Incorrect
1. 45,32<u>1</u>	ones	L	E
2. <u>7</u>10,486	hundred thousands	M	G
3. 438.<u>7</u>2	tens	Y	C
4. 6,7<u>5</u>8	tenths	P	W
5. <u>4</u>0,499,728	millions	T	P
6. 874.0<u>6</u>	hundredths	O	I
7. <u>1</u>,448,657	billions	A	H
8. 6.09<u>9</u>	thousandths	K	N
9. <u>3</u>5,420	ten thousands	C	H
10. 58,<u>2</u>75	hundreds	B	I
11. 0.0<u>9</u>8	tenths	E	J
12. <u>5</u>,793,652,000	trillions	R	X
13. 46<u>3</u>.2	tens	O	S
14. <u>2</u>,669,400	millions	L	G
15. <u>9</u>99,000.5	hundred thousands	P	L
16. 4.43<u>1</u>	hundreds	Y	A
17. 75.<u>7</u>8	tenths	W	P
18. <u>1</u>00,025	ten thousands	H	J
19. 5<u>9</u>,427.82	thousands	R	I
20. 6.1<u>0</u>3	hundredths	T	C
21. <u>1</u>00,007,500	hundred thousands	S	Q

The ancient number system is _____.

BRAINWORK: Research to find 5 facts about the number system revealed by your answers.

Name: _____ Power Skill: Comparing and ordering whole numbers

More or Less Than Meets the Eye

Casper the caterpillar eats more and more and feels less and less like moving. He dreams of a snug bed and of becoming more than currently meets the eye.

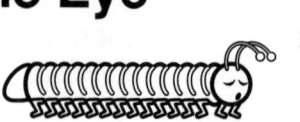

Compare the numbers in each section below to decide if the first number is *more than, less than,* or *equal to* the second number. Draw a <, >, or = in the circle between each set of numbers. Finally, use the color code and see Casper transformed before your eyes!

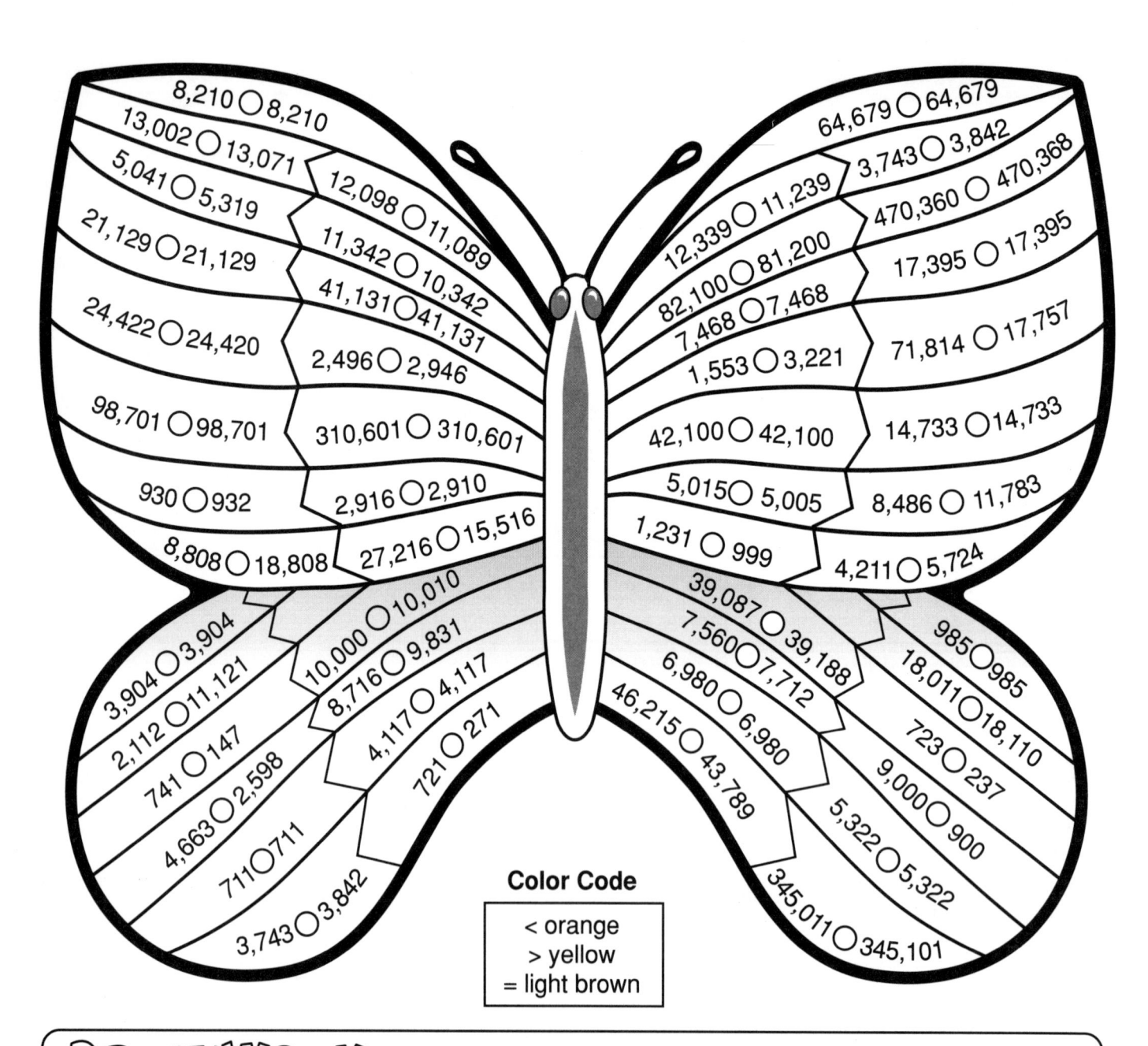

8,210 ○ 8,210
13,002 ○ 13,071
5,041 ○ 5,319
21,129 ○ 21,129
24,422 ○ 24,420
98,701 ○ 98,701
930 ○ 932
8,808 ○ 18,808
12,098 ○ 11,089
11,342 ○ 10,342
41,131 ○ 41,131
2,496 ○ 2,946
310,601 ○ 310,601
2,916 ○ 2,910
27,216 ○ 15,516

64,679 ○ 64,679
3,743 ○ 3,842
470,360 ○ 470,368
12,339 ○ 11,239
17,395 ○ 17,395
82,100 ○ 81,200
7,468 ○ 7,468
71,814 ○ 17,757
1,553 ○ 3,221
42,100 ○ 42,100
14,733 ○ 14,733
5,015 ○ 5,005
8,486 ○ 11,783
1,231 ○ 999
4,211 ○ 5,724

3,904 ○ 3,904
2,112 ○ 11,121
741 ○ 147
4,663 ○ 2,598
711 ○ 711
3,743 ○ 3,842
10,000 ○ 10,010
8,716 ○ 9,831
4,117 ○ 4,117
721 ○ 271

39,087 ○ 39,188
7,560 ○ 7,712
6,980 ○ 6,980
46,215 ○ 43,789

985 ○ 985
18,011 ○ 18,110
723 ○ 237
9,000 ○ 900
5,322 ○ 5,322
345,011 ○ 345,101

Color Code

< orange
> yellow
= light brown

BRAINWORK: On a separate sheet of paper, write down all the numbers in the yellow sections of the butterfly. Cut them apart, arrange them in order from least to greatest, and glue them onto the back of this sheet.

Name: _____   Power Skill: Comparing whole numbers and decimals

Prime-Time Swimmers

The regional swim meet finals are being televised. As an official, you have recorded the times of the swimmers in each event. Compare the times in each event. Then rank them from fastest to slowest so that results may be announced and medals awarded. Complete the charts below.

100-Meter Backstroke

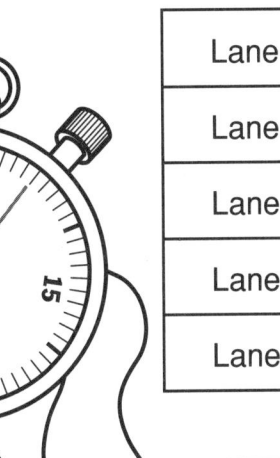

Lane 1	55.12
Lane 2	55.45
Lane 3	55.39
Lane 4	54.66
Lane 5	54.75

Place	Lane	Time
1st		
2nd		
3rd		
4th		
5th		

100-Meter Freestyle

Lane 1	48.52
Lane 2	49.10
Lane 3	48.95
Lane 4	48.59
Lane 5	49.01

Place	Lane	Time
1st		
2nd		
3rd		
4th		
5th		

100-Meter Butterfly

Lane 1	53.19
Lane 2	53.56
Lane 3	53.14
Lane 4	53.23
Lane 5	53.32

Place	Lane	Time
1st		
2nd		
3rd		
4th		
5th		

BRAINWORK: Write <, >, or = in each circle to compare the decimals.

28.026 ◯ 28.206   34.021 ◯ 34.0021   77.490 ◯ 77.409

©2001 The Education Center, Inc. • Power Practice • Math • TEC2667 • KEY p. 104

Name: _____ Power Skill: Classifying numbers

If the Shoe Fits

Five 3-footed aliens are shopping for shoes. The Best-Foot-Forward Shoe Shop seems to have enough shoes for them all, but it may be tricky to find just the right fit since every foot needs a different size. Each alien can only wear shoes in a particular category, as shown below. Some sizes will fit more than 1 alien, but there is only 1 solution that will meet the needs of all 5 aliens. Find a way to fit each foot. Work on scrap paper first to try different possibilities. Then write the correct answer on each alien's foot.

Shoe sizes available:

15	100	18	25	21
9	45	2	42	63
13	33	37	24	49

1st Alien: Odd number shoe sizes

2nd Alien: Prime number shoe sizes

3rd Alien: Squares of whole numbers shoe sizes

4th Alien: Multiples of 6 shoe sizes

5th Alien: Multiples of 9 shoe sizes

BRAINWORK: List all of the prime numbers from 1 to 50. (Hint: There are 15.)

Name: _____   Power Skill: Properties of integers

Food for Thought

Have you ever thought about the properties of integers? Well, if not, here's some food for thought!

If french fries are odd numbers and burgers are even numbers, what do you get when you add a french fry to a burger? Answer: French fry!

Test each equation below by inserting a sample number for each food. Solve the equation; then decide which food is the resulting answer—french fry (an odd number) or burger (an even number). Write your answer in the space provided.

1. french fry x french fry = _____
2. french fry x burger = _____
3. burger x burger = _____
4. burger + burger = _____
5. burger + french fry = _____
6. burger + burger + french fry = _____
7. 2-digit french fry ÷ 1-digit burger (drop the remainder) = _____

–10 –9 –8 –7 –6 –5 –4 –3 –2 –1 0 1 2 3 4 5 6 7 8 9 10

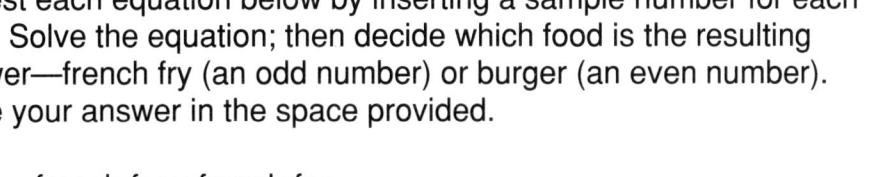

Integers include negative whole numbers, 0, and positive whole numbers, as shown on the number line. In the problems below, positive numbers are lettuce, negative numbers are tomatoes, and numbers that could be either positive or negative are carrots. Write the food that results from each operation with integers.

8. lettuce + lettuce = _____
9. tomato + tomato = _____
10. lettuce + tomato = _____
11. lettuce x tomato = _____
12. tomato x tomato = _____
13. tomato ÷ lettuce = _____
14. lettuce + tomato + lettuce = _____
15. tomato ÷ tomato = _____

BRAINWORK: On the back of this sheet, draw a sketch of a tomato plant that is 4 inches high. Show its roots growing 3 inches down into the soil. Then label your sketch with the integers that represent ground level, its depth below ground level, and its height above ground level.

©2001 The Education Center, Inc. • Power Practice • Math • TEC2667 • Key p. 104

Name: _____   Power Skill: Integers on a number line

Number Line of Scrimmage

The Central High Tigers and the Mountain High Lions are playing the last half of the most important football game of the season. Use the number line to find how many yards are gained or lost (the net yardage) on the following plays. Write the net yardage with a "+" in front of the number to show a gain and a "−" in front of the number to show a loss. Remember that 0 is always the line of scrimmage, your starting point.

−12 −11 −10 −9 −8 −7 −6 −5 −4 −3 −2 −1 0 +1 +2 +3 +4 +5 +6 +7 +8 +9 +10 +11 +12

1 Tiger's quarterback, Quentin, drops back 5 yards, then completes a 17-yard forward pass to Teddy Tightend. Net yardage: _____

2 On the next play, Quentin drops back 2 yards and hands off to Rowdy, who is rushed by the Lions, pushed back 4 more yards, and tackled. Net yardage: _____

3 On the third down, Quentin throws a 10-yard pass that slips through Rusty Receiver's hands. It is intercepted by Lucky Lion, who runs back 6 yards before he fumbles. The ball is recovered by the Tigers. Net yardage: _____

4 Puck the punter drops back 5 yards and only manages to kick the ball 15 yards, leaving the Lions in range to score. Net yardage: _____

5 Lions quarterback, Leo, throws a 7-yard forward pass to Lennie. He runs the ball 5 yards before he's pushed back 3 yards and tackled. Net yardage: _____

6 Quarterback Leo runs a keeper play and gains 8 yards, but he is really hit hard. He loses 4 yards as he's brought down by the Tigers defense. First down Lions! Net yardage: _____

7 On the next play, Leo drops back 4 yards and throws a 12-yard pass to Lennie, who leaps forward to gain another yard. Net yardage: _____

8 Leo drops back 8 yards looking for a receiver. Finally he runs, but only 3 yards. There's a fumble and the ball is recovered by the Tigers! Net yardage: _____

9 Time is running out as Quentin steps back a yard to throw. He launches a 12-yard pass. Rudy Runner makes a diving catch. Net yardage: _____

10 With only seconds remaining, Quentin breaks through the line and runs 6 yards before he makes a lateral pass to Hefty. Hefty powers on 6 yards across the goal line to score and clinch the win for the Tigers! Net yardage: _____

BRAINWORK: Use the net yardage answers above to find the total yardage of each team. Which team gained the most yardage in the second half of the game? _____

Name: _____   **Power Skill:** Ordering integers

Moving Day

Top of the Hill Town Houses is ready to open its newest complex. With moving trucks on the way, Arnold realizes that he has lost the box of number plates for the new houses. Help Arnold number the town houses correctly by following the directions below.

Directions: Look at the numbers below each row of houses. Order the house numbers from least to greatest. Then write the numbers on the houses in the spaces provided.

① 0, −4, +7, −3

② +2, 0, +3, −10

③ −14, 0, −6, +1

④ +5, −5, +12, −13

⑤ +20, −11, +4, −9

⑥ +19, −8, +11, −15

⑦ −21, +65, +40, −41

⑧ +100, +99, −98, +95

BRAINWORK: The Koglin house is built 5 feet below sea level. The Chance house is built 3 feet above sea level. Whose house is closer to sea level?

Name: _____   **Power Skill:** Properties of rational numbers

A Rationality Mentality

A new fad is sweeping the minds of the nation. Everyone's collecting rational number rings. Dinah, Armand, Sid, and Imogene plan to attend the Rational Number Ring Rally and display their collections. However, in order to enter their rings in the rally, they must classify each ring correctly. Follow the directions below to help this foursome with the task at hand.

Directions: A *rational number* is any number that can be expressed in the form $\frac{a}{b}$, where *a* is any integer and *b* is any integer except 0. Label each number ring below as a *whole number (WN)*, *integer (I)*, *fraction (F)*, or *decimal (D)*. Some may have more than one classification.

Rational Number Ring Rally

Dinah's Collection
5, $\frac{2}{4}$, −8, $\frac{13}{39}$, −6, 235, $5\frac{1}{8}$, $\frac{1}{7}$, 7.36

Armand's Collection
2.75, $\frac{2}{6}$, 78, $3\frac{5}{6}$, $\frac{13}{14}$, 40, −90, $5\frac{4}{5}$, $\frac{7}{8}$

Sid's Collection
6.9, −18, $\frac{6}{18}$, $32\frac{1}{5}$, 70, −11.3, $3\frac{3}{11}$, 11.77, $\frac{1}{5}$, 54

Imogene's Collection
$3\frac{1}{3}$, $\frac{3}{1}$, 30, $6\frac{1}{3}$, 4.77, −53, $12\frac{4}{5}$, 5.7, 77.88

BRAINWORK: On the back of this sheet, draw your own collection of rational number rings. Make yours bigger and better than any of the four rally contestants' rings above.

Name: _____ Power Skills: Comparing, ordering rational numbers

Pop It Into Place

Dig into the rational number sets in each bag of corny snacks below. Write the sets of rational numbers in order from least to greatest. Don't mix the popcorn with the caramel corn!

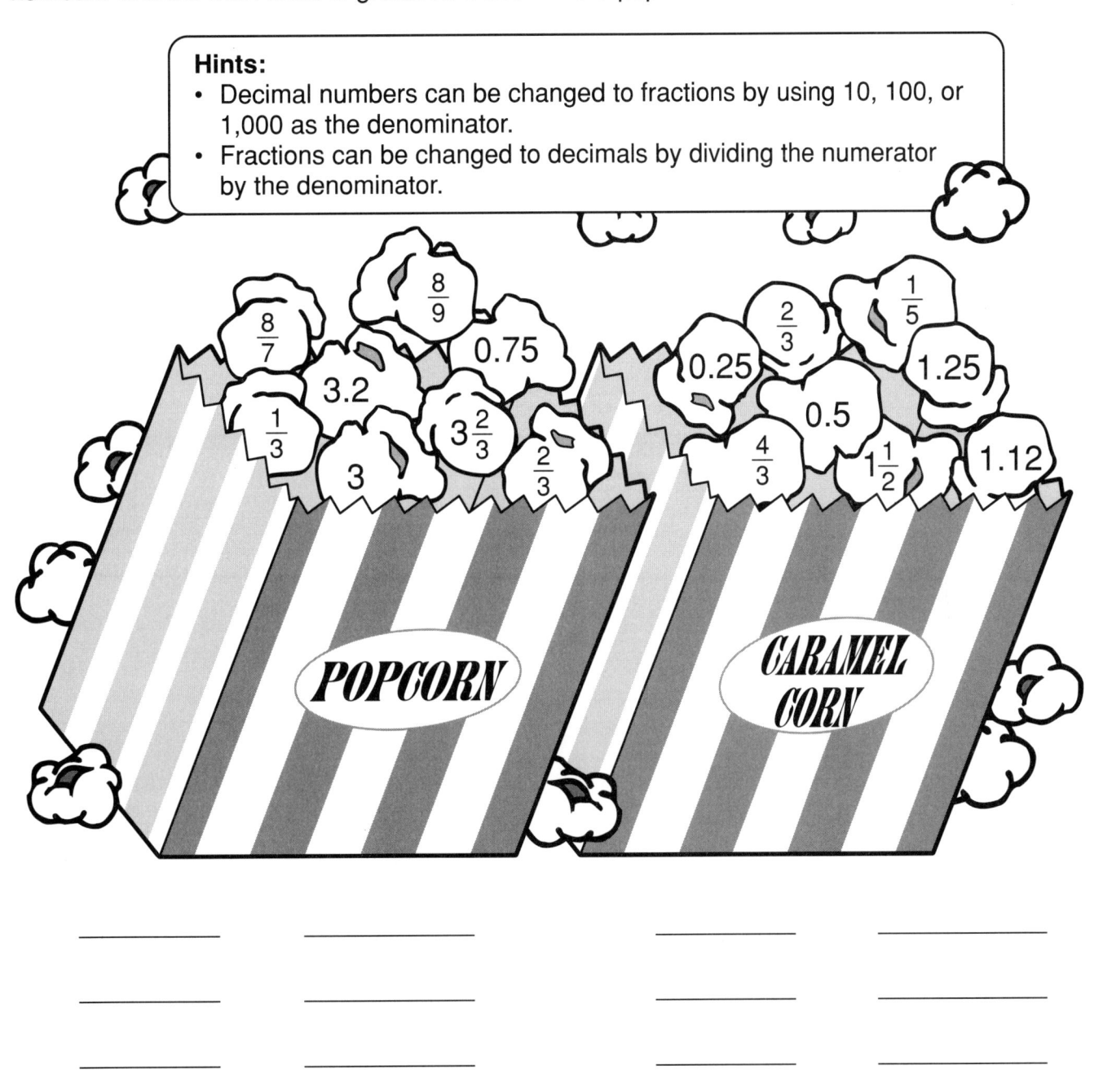

Hints:
- Decimal numbers can be changed to fractions by using 10, 100, or 1,000 as the denominator.
- Fractions can be changed to decimals by dividing the numerator by the denominator.

POPCORN: $\frac{8}{7}$, $\frac{8}{9}$, 0.75, 3.2, $\frac{1}{3}$, $3\frac{2}{3}$, 3, $\frac{2}{3}$

CARAMEL CORN: $\frac{2}{3}$, $\frac{1}{5}$, 0.25, 1.25, $\frac{4}{3}$, 0.5, $1\frac{1}{2}$, 1.12

_____ _____

_____ _____

_____ _____

_____ _____

BRAINWORK: For both the popcorn and caramel corn lists, write another rational number that is more than and one that is less than those in each list. Use fractions and decimals.

Name: _____ Power Skill: Finding squares and square roots

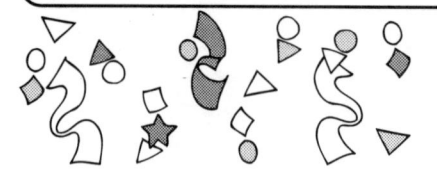

Getting a SQUARE Deal

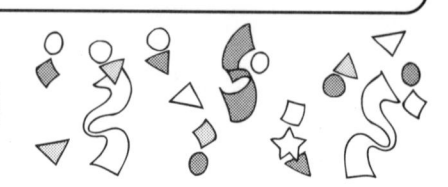

Want a square deal when it comes to solving riddles? This one's hard to beat!

Directions: Solve the problems to find the answer for each riddle below. Write the matching letter for each answer in the corresponding box. Shade in any unused boxes.

Riddle 1: What game did the 2 students play at recess?

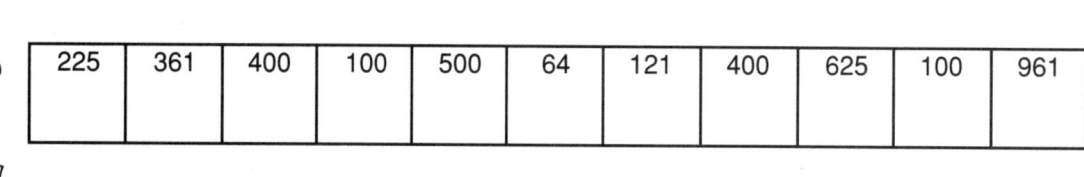

1. $8^2 = $ _____ (S)
2. $20^2 = $ _____ (U)
3. $10^2 = $ _____ (R)
4. $11^2 = $ _____ (Q)
5. $15^2 = $ _____ (F)
6. $19^2 = $ _____ (O)
7. $31^2 = $ _____ (E)
8. $25^2 = $ _____ (A)
9. $8^2 + 6^2 = $ _____ (R)
10. $4(10^2) = $ _____ (U)

| 225 | 361 | 400 | 100 | 500 | 64 | 121 | 400 | 625 | 100 | 961 |

Riddle 2: What did 10 say to 9 ?

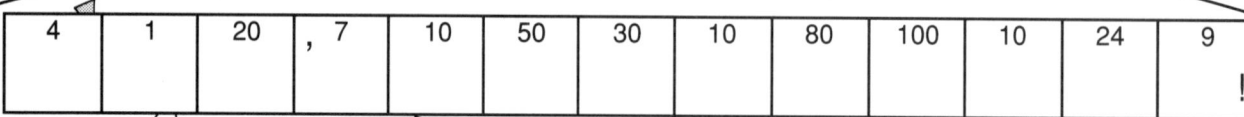

1. $\sqrt{49} = $ _____ (R)
2. $\sqrt{100} = $ _____ (E)
3. $\sqrt{81} = $ _____ (T)
4. $\sqrt{1} = $ _____ (O)
5. $\sqrt{400} = $ _____ (U)
6. $\sqrt{900} = $ _____ (P)
7. $\sqrt{576} = $ _____ (C)
8. $\sqrt{6{,}400} = $ _____ (R)
9. $\sqrt{10{,}000} = $ _____ (F)
10. $\sqrt{36 + 64} = $ _____ (E)
11. $\sqrt{25 - 9} = $ _____ (Y)
12. $\sqrt{25} + \sqrt{25} = $ _____ (E)

| 4 | 1 | 20 | , | 7 | 10 | 50 | 30 | 10 | 80 | 100 | 10 | 24 | 9 ! |

BRAINWORK: How many perfect squares are there from 1 to 200? List them on the back of this paper.

Name: _____ **Power Skill:** Adding whole numbers

Moneymaking Movie of the Week

The Reallybigshow Production Company is totaling the first week's profits from its latest hit movie, *Make Mars Mine*, which opened in several cities across the country. Find the sum of the total ticket sales for each region.

1. **NEW ENGLAND**
Bangor $14,587
Hartford $25,398
Montpelier $10,896
Boston $43,861

   Total: _____

2. **MIDDLE ATLANTIC**
New York $134,9870
Trenton $87,047
Philadelphia $49,087
Dover $12,842

   Total: _____

3. **SOUTHEAST**
Atlanta $104,486
Richmond $67,839
Charleston $49,012
Mobile $55,017

   Total: _____

4. **MIDWEST**
Cincinnati $87,981
Chicago $132,142
Kansas City $103,487

   Total: _____

5. **GREAT PLAINS**
Topeka $23,298
Bismarck $187,901
Omaha $35,871

   Total: _____

6. **ROCKY MOUNTAINS**
Denver $67,387
Salt Lake City $43,198
Phoenix $32,490
Albuquerque $12,139

   Total: _____

7. **WEST COAST**
Los Angeles $234,258
San Diego $146,209
San Francisco $98,076
Portland $78,378
Seattle $67,301

   Total: _____

8. **ALASKA & HAWAII**
Honolulu $23,209
Anchorage $13,298
Fairbanks $20,289

   Total: _____

BRAINWORK: Round each region's total to the nearest thousand. Then add to find the approximate total sales for the first week of *Make Mars Mine*.

Name: _____ Power Skill: Subtracting whole numbers

On the Road Again

Your favorite rock band, Mathematica, has just completed the first leg of a nationwide tour. To determine the frequent-traveler miles earned, the band's manager, Sauli D. Gold, needs help organizing the tour travel log pages below.

Use the distance chart and Mr. Gold's notes to fill in the missing information on each page. For example, on August 1, the band traveled from Boston to Atlanta. First, use the distance chart to find the distance between the 2 cities, which gives you the mileage for the day. Then subtract that distance from the ending mileage (82,219) to find the beginning mileage.

Distance Between Cities

	Atlanta	Boston	Houston	Nashville	Seattle
Atlanta	0	1,068	814	256	2,756
Boston	1,068	0	1,916	1,165	3,036
Houston	814	1,916	0	783	2,302
Nashville	256	1,165	783	0	2512
Seattle	2,756	3,036	2,302	2,512	0

Travel Log

The Mathematica Band

Boston, MA

Date: Aug. 1
From: Boston
To: Atlanta
Beginning mileage: _____
Ending mileage: 82,219
Mileage for the day: _____

Date: Aug. 4
From: _____
To: Nashville
Beginning mileage: 82,219
Ending mileage: 82,475
Mileage for the day: _____

Date: Aug. 6
From: Nashville
To: _____
Beginning mileage: _____
Ending mileage: 84,987
Mileage for the day: _____

Date: Aug. 8
From: Seattle
To: Atlanta
Beginning mileage: 84,987
Ending mileage: _____
Mileage for the day: _____

Date: Aug. 10
From: Atlanta
To: _____
Beginning mileage: _____
Ending mileage: 87,999
Mileage for the day: _____

Date: Aug. 12
From: _____
To: Houston
Beginning mileage: _____
Ending mileage: _____
Mileage for the day: _____

Date: Aug. 14
From: Houston
To: _____
Beginning mileage: 88,782
Ending mileage: 90,698
Mileage for the day: _____

BRAINWORK: How many miles did the band members travel from August 1 through August 14? How many more miles must they travel to reach the frequent traveler goal of 10,000 miles?

16   ©2001 The Education Center, Inc. • Power Practice • Math • TEC2667 • Key p. 105

Name: _____

Power Skill: Subtracting across zeros

Submerged in Subtraction

Submerge yourself in subtraction by following the directions below.

Directions: Study the example. Then subtract across zeros to solve each problem below. Check your answers as shown on the example. For each subtraction problem, color the submarine that shows the correct answer. Then write the letter in the submarine on the corresponding line below to find out which type of submarine doesn't like the city.

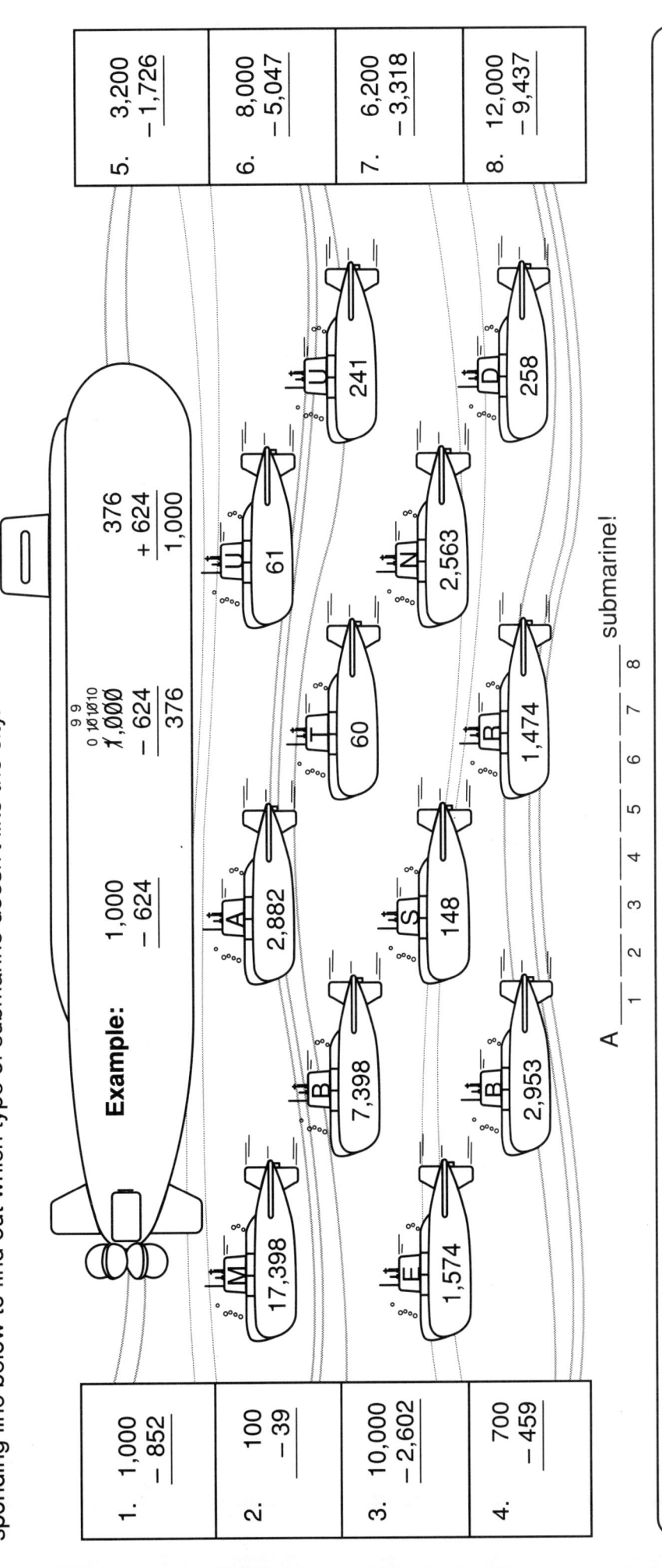

Example:

```
         9 9
      0 10 10 10
      1,0 0 0        376
      -  624       + 624
      ———         ———
         376       1,000
```

1. 1,000
   − 852

2. 100
   − 39

3. 10,000
   − 2,602

4. 700
   − 459

5. 3,200
   − 1,726

6. 8,000
   − 5,047

7. 6,200
   − 3,318

8. 12,000
   − 9,437

Submarines:
M 17,398
B 7,398
A 2,882
61
60
U 241
E 1,574
E 1,574
S 148
T ...
N 2,563
D 258
B 2,953
B 1,474

A ___ ___ ___ ___ ___ ___ ___ ___ submarine!
   1   2   3   4   5   6   7   8

BRAINWORK! Draw a large submarine on the top half of another sheet of paper. Inside the submarine, write a subtraction problem that has a minuend ending with six 0s. On the bottom half draw another submarine and write the answer inside. Fold the answer under and then give your problem to a friend to solve.

17

Name: _____   **Power Skill:** Estimating

Party Favor Wish Lists

Jillian plans to celebrate her birthday with a party at Skate Station. For party favors, she's decided to let each guest choose 4 trinkets from the Skate Station Store. She has asked guests to write down the 4 items they'd like.

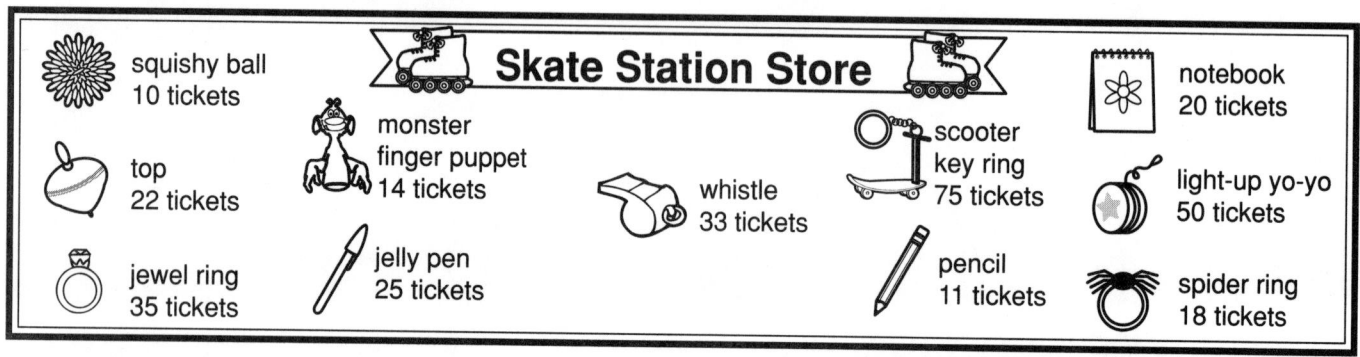

Skate Station Store

- squishy ball — 10 tickets
- top — 22 tickets
- jewel ring — 35 tickets
- monster finger puppet — 14 tickets
- jelly pen — 25 tickets
- whistle — 33 tickets
- scooter key ring — 75 tickets
- pencil — 11 tickets
- notebook — 20 tickets
- light-up yo-yo — 50 tickets
- spider ring — 18 tickets

Part 1: Below is a list of the 4 items each guest has chosen. Write the number of tickets needed for each item on each guest's wish list. Then estimate the total number of tickets for each guest by rounding each number to the greatest place-value position (in this case, the nearest ten).

1. Laurie's Wish List
   _____ top
   _____ jelly pen
   _____ light-up yo-yo
   _____ spider ring   about ____ tickets

2. Sammy's Wish List
   _____ scooter keyring
   _____ light-up yo-yo
   _____ pencil
   _____ whistle   about ____ tickets

3. Francesca's Wish List
   _____ jelly pen
   _____ jewel ring
   _____ scooter keyring
   _____ squishy ball   about ____ tickets

4. Jessica's Wish List
   _____ whistle
   _____ notebook
   _____ spider ring
   _____ jelly pen   about ____ tickets

5. Dylan's Wish List
   _____ squishy ball
   _____ light-up yo-yo
   _____ monster finger puppet
   _____ whistle   about ____ tickets

6. Nick's Wish List
   _____ top
   _____ spider ring
   _____ light-up yo-yo
   _____ whistle   about ____ tickets

Jillian will need about ____ tickets in all.

Part 2: If each ticket costs $0.05, about how much money will Jillian need to purchase the tickets for her friends' party favors? Round your answer to the nearest dollar. Jillian will need about $_____.

BRAINWORK: Can you estimate the number of days until your birthday? If you assume each month has about 30 days, it should be easy. After you have an answer, use a calendar to count the actual number of days. How close was your estimation?

18   ©2001 The Education Center, Inc. • Power Practice • Math • TEC2667 • Key p. 105

Name: _____ Power Skill: Multiplying whole numbers

The Mighty Megastack Burger

Benny's Burger Bar features many delicious and unique burgers. This month's burger special is the Mighty Megastack Burger. Help Benny complete his advertisement below. First, solve each multiplication problem. Next, match each answer with 1 of the burger's stacked ingredients. Then color each answer as indicated.

#	Problem	Color
1.	156 × 12	purple
2.	255 × 15	brown
3.	368 × 23	red
4.	132 × 26	brown
5.	329 × 16	green
6.	231 × 22	brown

Burger stack (top to bottom): 4,137 ; 5,264 ; 1,872 ; 4,784 ; 2,870 ; 3,825 ; 8,464 ; 9,889 ; 3,432 ; 5,700 ; 4,770 ; 5,082

#	Problem	Color
7.	368 × 13	red
8.	265 × 18	green
9.	197 × 21	brown
10.	205 × 14	green
11.	341 × 29	orange
12.	475 × 12	purple

BRAINWORK: Every customer who buys a Mighty Megastack Burger will receive a bumper sticker that says "Attack a Stack at Benny's Burger Bar." Each bumper sticker requires 12 inches of plastic sticker tape. If Benny expects to sell 675 Mighty Megastack Burgers, how many inches of sticker tape will be needed?

Name: _____   **Power Skill:** Multiplying by 3 digits

Faulty Advertising?

Billions of Bubbles, Inc., could be in trouble! Its TV commercial promises that kids can blow billions of bubbles in an hour by using any of its magic wands and secret bubble mixture. Parents are complaining that this claim is false. Calculate the data below (obtained randomly from the kids themselves) to find out whether this company needs to change its ad!

Deluxe—up to 436 bubbles!
Super Deluxe—up to 738 bubbles!
Extreme Deluxe—up to 947 bubbles!
Super Extreme Deluxe—up to 963 bubbles!

You'll blow BILLIONS of bubbles in an hour with our wands and special bubble solution! See for yourself how many bubbles are possible with each magic bubble wand!

1. Bubble wand: **Deluxe**
Number of uses in 1 hour: 484
Total bubbles: _____

2. Bubble wand: **Deluxe**
Number of uses in 1 hour: 149
Total bubbles: _____

3. Bubble wand: **Super Deluxe**
Number of uses in 1 hour: 752
Total bubbles: _____

4. Bubble wand: **Super Deluxe**
Number of uses in 1 hour: 841
Total bubbles: _____

5. Bubble wand: **Extreme Deluxe**
Number of uses in 1 hour: 236
Total bubbles: _____

6. Bubble wand: **Extreme Deluxe**
Number of uses in 1 hour: 542
Total bubbles: _____

7. Bubble wand: **Extreme Deluxe**
Number of uses in 1 hour: 560
Total bubbles: _____

8. Bubble wand: **Super Extreme Deluxe**
Number of uses in 1 hour: 317
Total bubbles: _____

BRAINWORK: Based on your calculations, should Billions of Bubbles, Inc., change its ad? Why or why not?

Name: _____   **Power Skill:** Dividing whole numbers

Great Blocks of Division

Have you ever walked a mile? How about 4,000 miles? That is the length of the longest structure ever built. To find out its name, step your way through the division problems below. Use the back of the page to work the problems. Then match your answers to the numbers at the bottom of the page and write the corresponding letter on the blank. *(Hint: You will not use every letter.)*

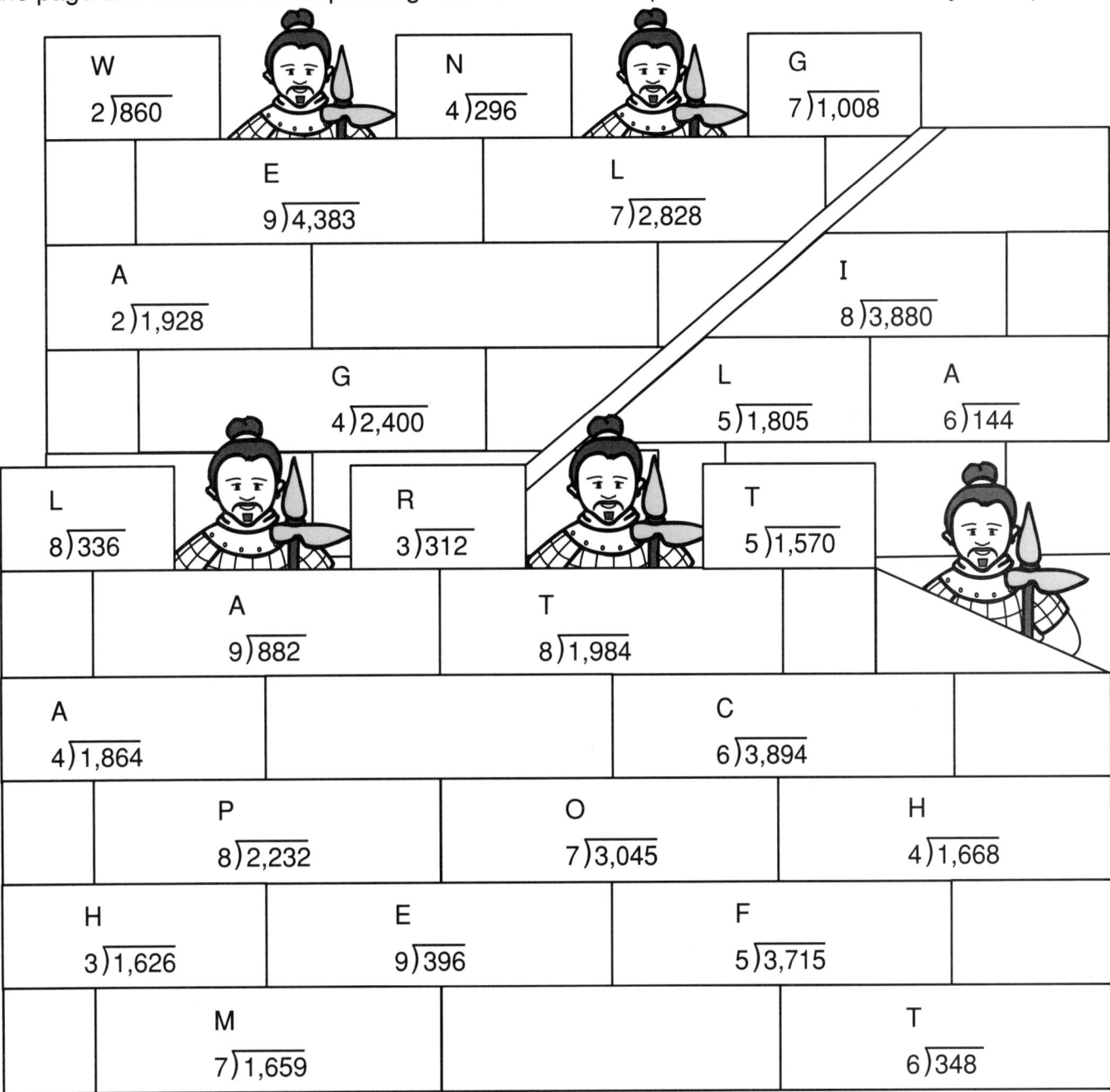

W 2)860
N 4)296
G 7)1,008
E 9)4,383
L 7)2,828
A 2)1,928
I 8)3,880
G 4)2,400
L 5)1,805
A 6)144
L 8)336
R 3)312
T 5)1,570
A 9)882
T 8)1,984
A 4)1,864
C 6)3,894
P 8)2,232
O 7)3,045
H 4)1,668
H 3)1,626
E 9)396
F 5)3,715
M 7)1,659
T 6)348

What is the longest structure ever built?

___ ___ ___   ___ ___ ___ ___   ___ ___ ___ ___   ___ ___ ___   ___ ___ ___ ___
248 417 487   144 104 44 466 314   430 24 42 404   435 743   649 542 485 74 964

BRAINWORK: If the emperor builds a guard tower every 8 miles, how many towers will he build? If the emperor has 3,000 warriors, how many can he post at each tower?

Name: _____   Power Skill: Dividing whole numbers with remainders

On the Continental Divide Trail

The Continental Divide Trail winds for 3,000 miles along the crest of the Continental Divide, from the Canadian border to the Mexican border. Solve each problem below. Then connect the dots of the remainders to complete the trail from north to south.

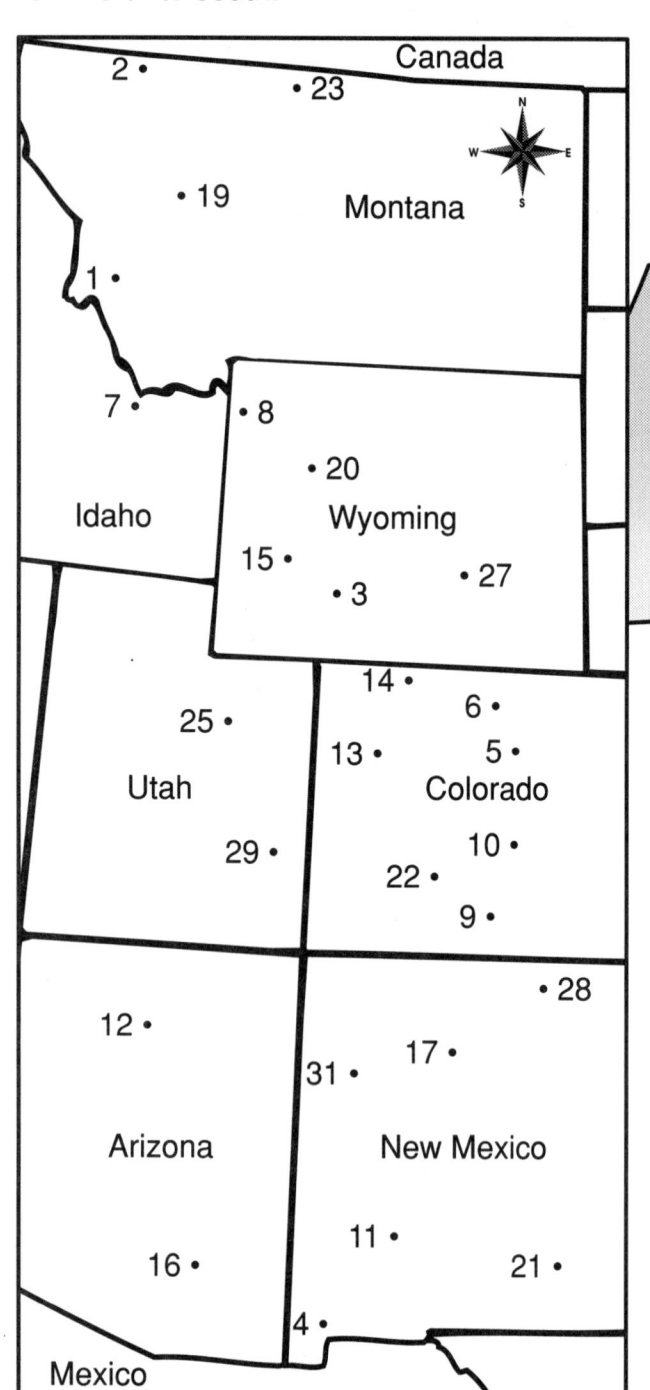

① 38 ÷ 11 = _____   ② 49 ÷ 5 = _____
③ 97 ÷ 8 = _____   ④ 82 ÷ 12 = _____
⑤ 59 ÷ 12 = _____   ⑥ 71 ÷ 8 = _____
⑦ 39 ÷ 10 = _____   ⑧ 98 ÷ 6 = _____
⑨ 122 ÷ 25 = _____   ⑩ 68 ÷ 10 = _____
⑪ 63 ÷ 4 = _____   ⑫ 79 ÷ 20 = _____
⑬ 74 ÷ 15 = _____   ⑭ 140 ÷ 30 = _____
⑮ 117 ÷ 20 = _____   ⑯ 62 ÷ 7 = _____

BRAINWORK: Harry and Julia plan to hike the entire Continental Divide Trail. If they average 11 miles a day, how many days will it take to complete the 3,000-mile journey?

Power Skill: Dividing with 2-digit divisors

Divvyin' Up the Goods

Dave and Deedee work in the shipping department at Donnavan's Packing Company. Follow the directions to help them package the orders below.

Directions: Each dividend tells the number of items ordered. Each divisor tells the number of items of that type that can be packed in each box. For each order, shade the box labeled with the more reasonable estimate of boxes needed. Next, divide to check your estimate. Show your work on another sheet of paper and record the exact quotient on the box shape provided. Write the total boxes needed on the last box shape. The first one has been done for you.

	Order	Estimate		Exact	Total
1.	100 ÷ 33	3	30	3 R 1	4
2.	613 ÷ 72	95	8		
3.	547 ÷ 86	4	6		
4.	1,932 ÷ 35	55	40		
5.	730 ÷ 16	30	45		
6.	80 ÷ 37	2	20		
7.	317 ÷ 79	30	4		
8.	786 ÷ 52	15	100		
9.	4,581 ÷ 32	105	140		
10.	1,985 ÷ 23	80	70		
11.	5,401 ÷ 25	20	200		
12.	6,014 ÷ 97	60	600		
13.	279 ÷ 34	8	80		
14.	758 ÷ 65	11	90		

BRAINWORK: Find the total number of boxes Dave and Deedee will need to fill all 14 orders.

Name: _____   Power Skill: Equivalent fractions, decimals, percentages

It's All the Same to Me!

Welcome to the third annual Game Day on Planet Equi-zorf! You are in charge of gathering each team of three aliens together. Find each set of equivalent fractions, decimals, and percentages. Then color the flags the same color.

0.75	$\frac{3}{50}$	$\frac{1}{4}$	0.625	50%	$\frac{7}{10}$
$\frac{18}{100}$	$\frac{2}{5}$	$\frac{3}{4}$	0.7	20%	0.55
$\frac{1}{2}$	0.2	$\frac{5}{8}$	75%	0.4	$\frac{11}{20}$
6%	0.25	18%	40%	0.5	70%
55%	62.5%	$\frac{1}{5}$	0.06	0.18	25%

BRAINWORK: Create another set of triplets showing an equivalent fraction, decimal, and percentage. Draw a picture of the triplets on the back of this page.

Name: _____ **Power Skill:** Adding like fractions

A Slice of the Pie

Like fractions are fractions that have the same denominator. To add like fractions, add only the numerators. Then write the denominator.

Directions: Add the fractions. Reduce the sum to its lowest terms, when necessary. Next, find the pie that matches the answer. Then write the letter to the corresponding problem number below to answer the riddle at the bottom of the page.

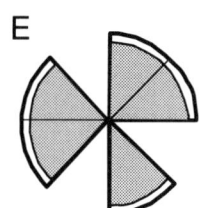

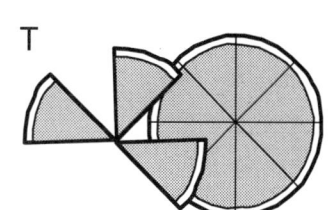

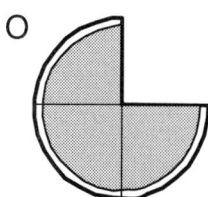

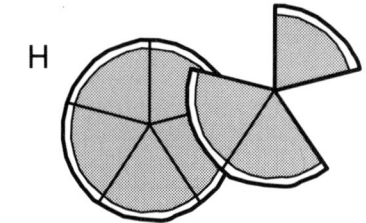

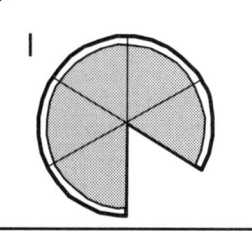

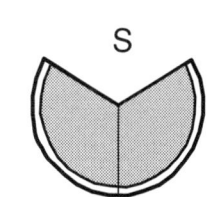

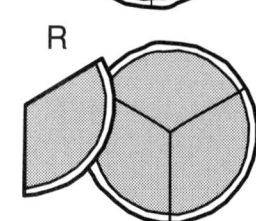

E   T   O

H   I   S   R

1. $\frac{2}{5} + \frac{1}{5} =$ _____

2. $\frac{2}{6} + \frac{3}{6} =$ _____

3. $\frac{2}{7} + \frac{4}{7} =$ _____

4. $\frac{1}{4} + \frac{2}{4} =$ _____

5. $\frac{4}{9} + \frac{2}{9} =$ _____ = _____

6. $\frac{3}{8} + \frac{2}{8} =$ _____

7. $\frac{3}{6} + \frac{5}{6} =$ _____ = _____

8. $\frac{3}{4} + \frac{3}{4} =$ _____ = _____

9. $\frac{5}{8} + \frac{6}{8} =$ _____ = _____

10. $\frac{4}{5} + \frac{4}{5} =$ _____ = _____

11. $\frac{2}{9} + \frac{7}{9} =$ _____ = _____

12. $\frac{5}{6} + \frac{5}{6} =$ _____ = _____

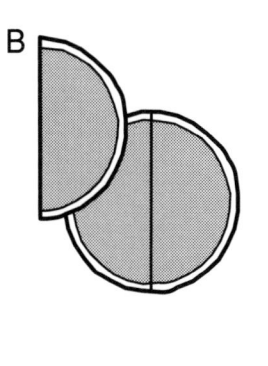

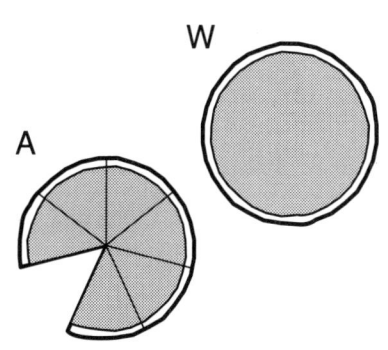

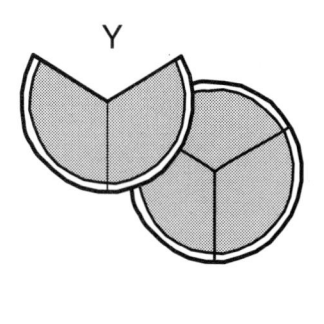

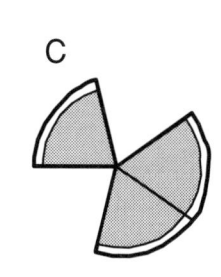

B   W   Y   A   C

What is a monster's favorite dessert?

___ ___ ___ - ___ ___ ___ ___ ___   ___ P ___   ___ ___ ___ ___   ___ - ___ ___ ___ ___ ___ M !
 8   4   4   8   6   7   7 12   2   6   11 2   9 10   2   5   1   7   6   3

BRAINWORK: Imagine that there were no more fractions. How would this affect a baker's job?

©2001 The Education Center, Inc. • Power Practice • Math • TEC2667 • Key p. 105   25

Power Skill: Adding mixed numbers

Fishy Fractions

Add the mixed numbers correctly to make Freddy Fish's reflection appear!

Directions: Add to solve each problem below. Write each answer in lowest terms. Then cut out the puzzle pieces below. Glue each piece in the space with the matching answer.

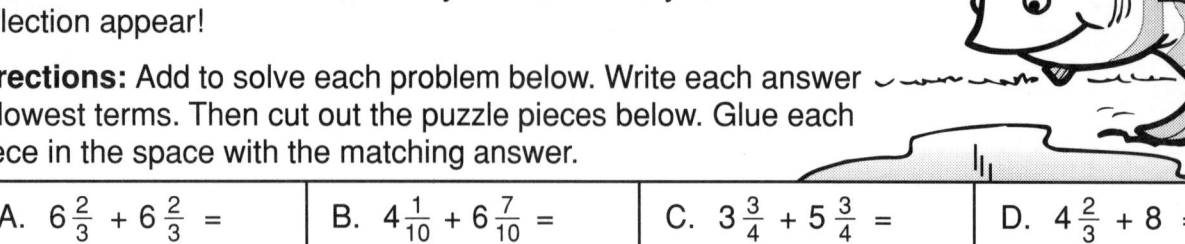

A. $6\frac{2}{3} + 6\frac{2}{3} =$	B. $4\frac{1}{10} + 6\frac{7}{10} =$	C. $3\frac{3}{4} + 5\frac{3}{4} =$	D. $4\frac{2}{3} + 8 =$
E. $4\frac{1}{8} + 4\frac{1}{8} =$	F. $3\frac{1}{8} + 4\frac{3}{8} =$	G. $6\frac{1}{3} + 1 =$	H. $6\frac{5}{8} + 4\frac{3}{8} =$
I. $9\frac{7}{10} + 9\frac{1}{10} =$	J. $4\frac{2}{15} + \frac{8}{15} =$	K. $2\frac{17}{20} + 4\frac{7}{20} =$	L. $4\frac{2}{3} + 10\frac{1}{3} =$
M. $4\frac{1}{10} + 8\frac{3}{10} =$	N. $5\frac{5}{6} + 2\frac{5}{6} =$	O. $7\frac{4}{5} + 5\frac{3}{5} =$	P. $12\frac{1}{4} + 5\frac{3}{4} =$

BRAINWORK: I am a mixed number in lowest terms. My denominator is the greatest common factor of 12 and 18. I am greater than 8, but less than $8\frac{1}{2}$. What number am I?

©2001 The Education Center, Inc. • Power Practice • Math • TEC2667 • Key p. 106

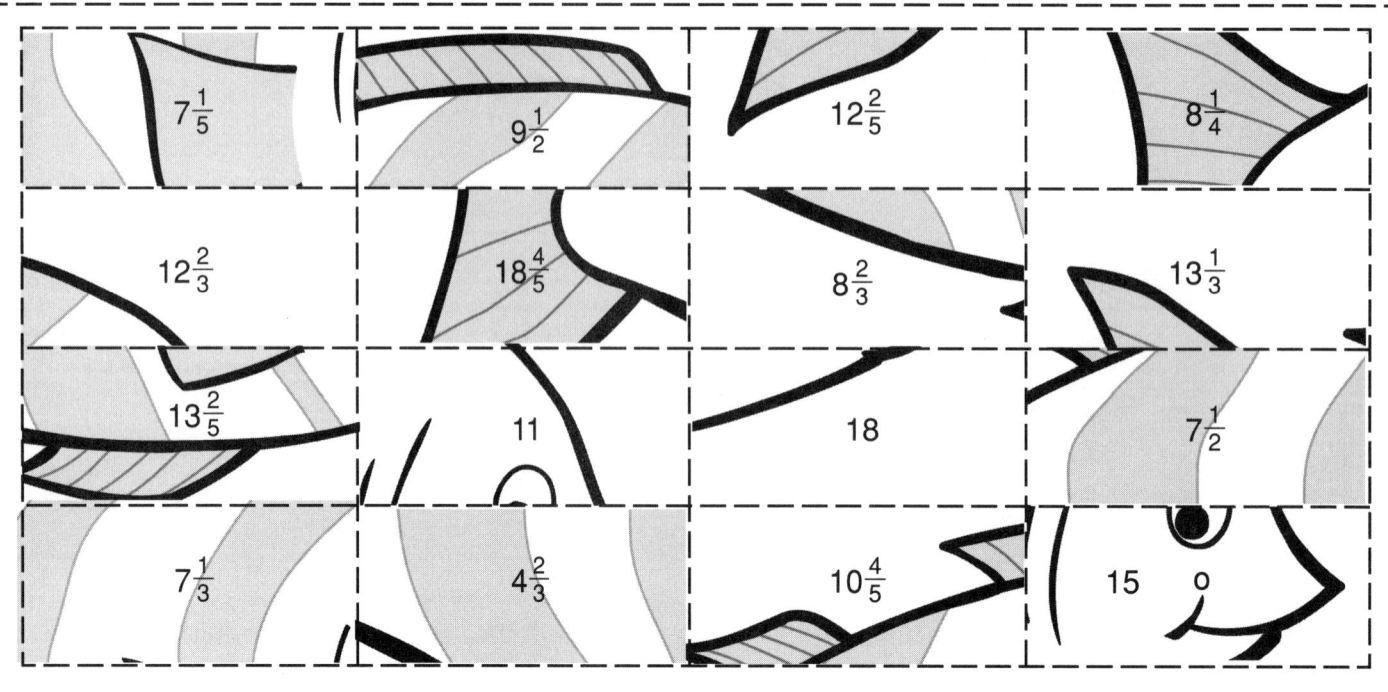

Puzzle pieces:

$7\frac{1}{5}$ | $9\frac{1}{2}$ | $12\frac{2}{5}$ | $8\frac{1}{4}$

$12\frac{2}{3}$ | $18\frac{4}{5}$ | $8\frac{2}{3}$ | $13\frac{1}{3}$

$13\frac{2}{5}$ | 11 | 18 | $7\frac{1}{2}$

$7\frac{1}{3}$ | $4\frac{2}{3}$ | $10\frac{4}{5}$ | 15

26 **Note to the teacher:** Provide each student with glue and scissors to assemble the puzzle.

Name: _____   Power Skill: Subtracting fractions

Piggy Portions

Papa Pig ordered a pizza for each member of his family. Each pig ate a portion of its pizza for breakfast, lunch, and dinner. Write a subtraction sentence showing how much pizza was eaten at each meal. Then shade the pizza to show how much was eaten in all. Next, write the fractional amount of leftover pizza in lowest terms. The first one has been done for you.

1. Papa Pig
   $\frac{2}{8}$ for breakfast $\frac{8}{8} - \frac{2}{8} = \frac{6}{8}$
   $\frac{3}{8}$ for lunch $\frac{6}{8} - \frac{3}{8} = \frac{3}{8}$
   $\frac{1}{8}$ for dinner $\frac{3}{8} - \frac{1}{8} = \frac{2}{8}$

   Fractional amount left $\frac{1}{4}$

2. Mama Pig
   $\frac{2}{6}$ for breakfast _____
   $\frac{1}{6}$ for lunch _____
   $\frac{2}{6}$ for dinner _____

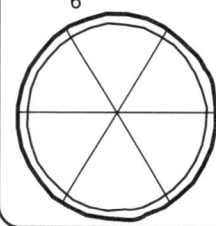

   Fractional amount left _____

3. Paula Pig
   $\frac{3}{10}$ for breakfast _____
   $\frac{1}{10}$ for lunch _____
   $\frac{4}{10}$ for dinner _____

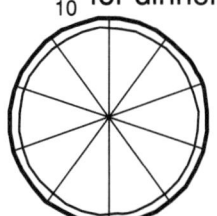

   Fractional amount left _____

4. Pete Pig
   $\frac{3}{9}$ for breakfast _____
   $\frac{2}{9}$ for lunch _____
   $\frac{1}{9}$ for dinner _____

   Fractional amount left _____

5. Pedro Pig
   $\frac{1}{12}$ for breakfast _____
   $\frac{3}{12}$ for lunch _____
   $\frac{2}{12}$ for dinner _____

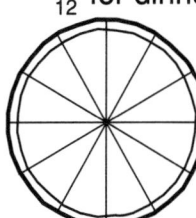

   Fractional amount left _____

6. Penelope Pig
   $\frac{3}{16}$ for breakfast _____
   $\frac{5}{16}$ for lunch _____
   $\frac{6}{16}$ for dinner _____

   Fractional amount left _____

BRAINWORK: On the back of this page, list the pigs' leftovers from least to greatest.

Name: _____　　　　　　**Power Skill:** Multiplying fractions

Soccer Savvy

Directions for each problem:
1. Use a red crayon to color the rows that represent the first fraction.
2. Use a yellow crayon to color the columns that represent the second fraction.
3. Count the boxes that are shaded with both colors. Write the fractional amount in the space provided. Then, if possible, reduce your answer to the lowest term. The first one has been done for you.

1. 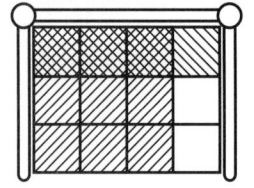 $\frac{1}{3} \times \frac{3}{4} = \frac{3}{12} = \frac{1}{4}$

2. 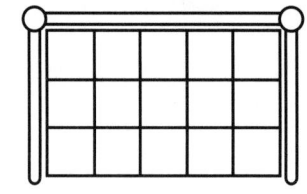 $\frac{2}{3} \times \frac{2}{5} =$ _____

3. 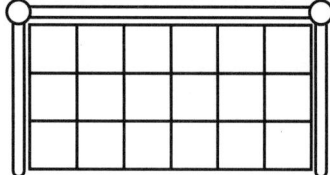 $\frac{1}{3} \times \frac{5}{6} =$ _____

4. 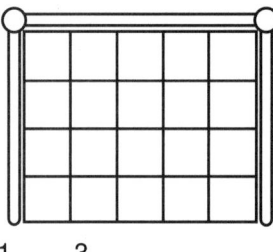 $\frac{1}{4} \times \frac{3}{5} =$ _____

5. 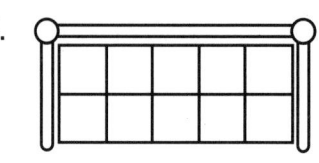 $\frac{1}{2} \times \frac{2}{5} =$ _____

6. 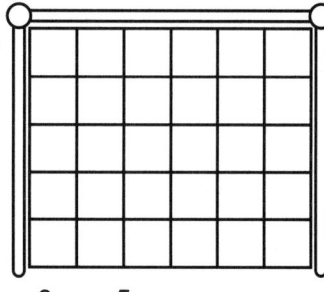 $\frac{3}{5} \times \frac{5}{6} =$ _____

7. 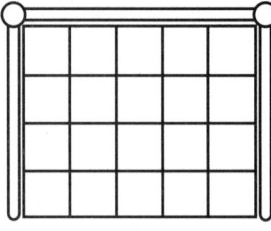 $\frac{3}{4} \times \frac{3}{5} =$ _____

8. 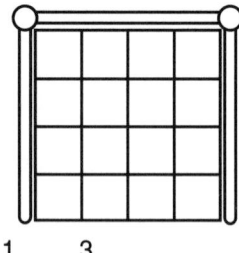 $\frac{1}{4} \times \frac{3}{4} =$ _____

9. 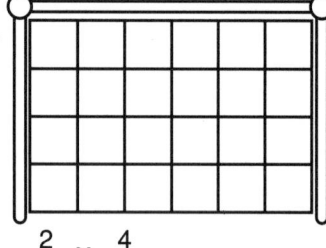 $\frac{2}{4} \times \frac{4}{6} =$ _____

10. 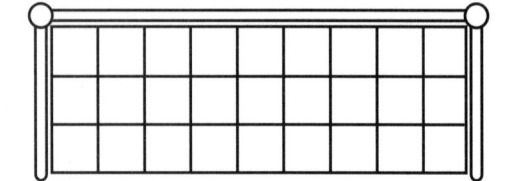 $\frac{1}{3} \times \frac{4}{9} =$ _____

BRAINWORK: Draw a soccer net similar to the ones above to multiply $\frac{3}{4}$ and $\frac{5}{8}$. Color the boxes in the net to find the answer.

Name: _____   Power Skill: Dividing fractions

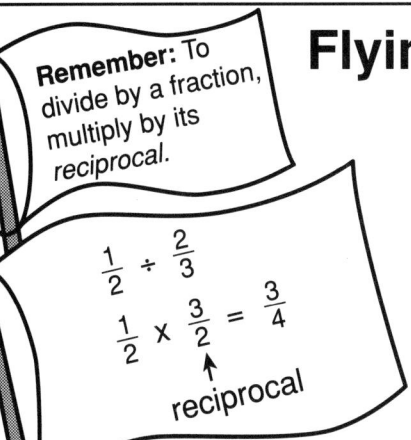

Flying High With Fractions

Remember: To divide by a fraction, multiply by its *reciprocal*.

$\frac{1}{2} \div \frac{2}{3}$
$\frac{1}{2} \times \frac{3}{2} = \frac{3}{4}$
↑ reciprocal

Let your division skills fly high as you discover the colors of these national flags! Divide each fraction below. Find the answer on the color code. Then color the stripes on the flag accordingly.

Color Code

Blue	=	$\frac{3}{4}$
Black	=	1
White	=	$\frac{4}{5}$
Red	=	$\frac{1}{2}$
Yellow	=	$1\frac{1}{2}$
Green	=	2

1. Estonia
   $\frac{1}{4} \div \frac{1}{3} =$ _____
   $\frac{3}{4} \div \frac{3}{4} =$ _____
   $\frac{1}{4} \div \frac{5}{16} =$ _____

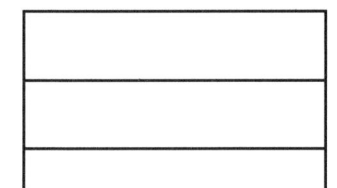

2. Netherlands
   $\frac{3}{10} \div \frac{3}{5} =$ _____
   $\frac{2}{5} \div \frac{1}{2} =$ _____
   $\frac{1}{2} \div \frac{2}{3} =$ _____

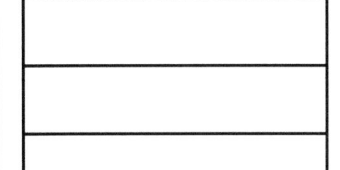

3. Colombia
   $\frac{1}{2} \div \frac{1}{3} =$ _____
   $\frac{1}{3} \div \frac{4}{9} =$ _____
   $\frac{3}{10} \div \frac{3}{5} =$ _____

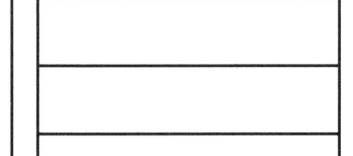

4. Ethiopia
   $\frac{2}{5} \div \frac{1}{5} =$ _____
   $\frac{3}{8} \div \frac{1}{4} =$ _____
   $\frac{1}{12} \div \frac{1}{6} =$ _____

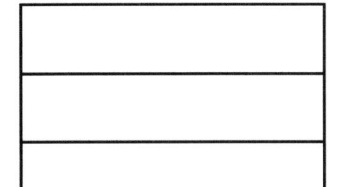

5. Bulgaria
   $\frac{4}{5} \div \frac{2}{2} =$ _____
   $\frac{1}{2} \div \frac{1}{4} =$ _____
   $\frac{1}{2} \div \frac{3}{3} =$ _____

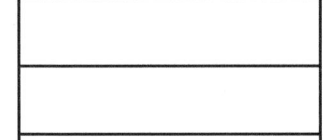

6. Yemen
   $\frac{2}{7} \div \frac{4}{7} =$ _____
   $\frac{7}{10} \div \frac{7}{8} =$ _____
   $\frac{3}{12} \div \frac{1}{4} =$ _____

7. Sierra Leone
   $\frac{1}{3} \div \frac{1}{6} =$ _____
   $\frac{3}{5} \div \frac{3}{4} =$ _____
   $\frac{1}{12} \div \frac{1}{9} =$ _____

8. Hungary
   $\frac{5}{6} \div \frac{5}{3} =$ _____
   $\frac{1}{3} \div \frac{5}{12} =$ _____
   $\frac{1}{8} \div \frac{1}{16} =$ _____

BRAINWORK: Design a fraction flag problem similar to the ones above. Give it to a classmate to solve.

Name: _____   Power Skill: Adding and subtracting money

Valley Town Video

Vince is a new cashier at Valley Town Video. With all the costs of videos, late fees, and deductions for coupons, he is having trouble calculating how much to charge each customer. Now his checkout line is getting longer, and the boss is watching! Help Vince by listing and finding the charges for each customer on each receipt below. The first one has been started for you.

1.
- Galaxy Wars (H)
- Paul the Penguin (C)
- Gotcha! (G)
- ★ Coupon

$ 4.29
3.33
3.88
$
Coupon − 1.00
Total $

Valley Town Video
Rental fees:
- (H) Hot New Choices $4.29
- (L) Good for a Laugh $3.75
- (O) Oldies but Goodies $3.89
- (C) Children's Picks $3.33
- (G) Games $3.88
- (I) Informational $2.77

Late fees: $2.25 per day

Coupon codes:
★ $1.00 off
☺ Cheapest video free
$ $0.75 off each video

2.
- Gourmet Cook (I)
- Tornado! (H)
- State Your Case (O)
- Late fee: 1 day

3.
- What's Up With Joe? (O)
- Sing-Along Songs (C)
- All Eyes Are Watching! (H)
- Square Deal (G)
- Late fee: 2 days
- ☺ Coupon

4.
- Raising Rabbits (I)
- My Friend Freida (O)
- $ Coupon

5.
- How to Install a Sink (I)
- Comical Capers (L)
- Topsy Turvy! (L)
- ★ Coupon

6.
- The Missing Movie Mogul (L)
- Greek Culture (I)
- Davy the Dinosaur (C)
- Get to the Top (I)
- Late fee: 1 day
- ☺ Coupon

7.
- Wally Wonder Dog (I)
- Outlaw (G)
- How to Be a Better Golfer (I)

BRAINWORK: Pretend you are renting one video for each member of your family. Select the type of video each family member would enjoy most. If you owe no late fees and have one coupon (your choice), what would your total charges be?

Name: _____   Power Skill: Multiplying decimals

Jogging Mugsy's Memory

Mugsy, Matt's mutt, has forgotten where his favorite bone is buried. He knows it's buried in one of the holes A through L below. Help him find his bone by following the directions below.

Directions: Multiply the problems below on another sheet of paper. Write the product of each problem on the line provided. Write the number of decimal places in each product in the circle provided. Remember, sometimes zeros must be added to a product to show the correct number of decimal places (see the example)! Then read the clue at the bottom of the page to reveal where Mugsy's favorite bone is buried.

```
  0.34    2 decimal places
x 0.08   +2 decimal places
 0.0272   4 decimal places
```

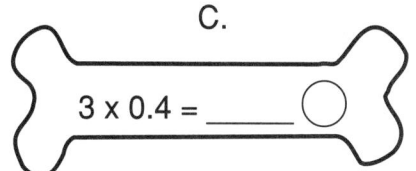

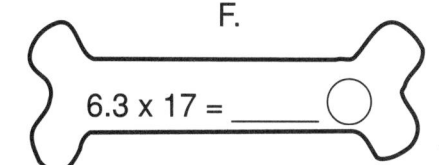

A. 0.2 x 0.3 = _____ ◯

B. 0.82 x 0.3 = _____ ◯

C. 3 x 0.4 = _____ ◯

D. 0.23 x 9.4 = _____ ◯

E. 0.36 x 0.01 = _____ ◯

F. 6.3 x 17 = _____ ◯

G. 2.1 x 1.4 = _____ ◯

H. 0.5 x 0.5 = _____ ◯

I. 1.03 x 7 = _____ ◯

J. 0.21 x 0.3 = _____ ◯

K. 0.49 x 0.12 = _____ ◯

L. 0.9 x 14 = _____ ◯

Clue: Mugsy can find his favorite bone at hole _____ (where the sum of the product's digits is 15).

BRAINWORK: Multiply the products of the problems above in this pattern: A x B, C x D, E x F, G x H, I x J, and K x L.

©2001 The Education Center, Inc. • Power Practice • Math • TEC2667 • Key p. 106   31

Name: _____ Power Skill: Dividing decimals by whole numbers

Dinah's Decimal Dilemma

Dinah's really done it this time! She's moved the decimals in the answers that will be used in the next round of her school's annual Decimal IQ Bowl. She *must* find the exact location of the decimals before this round begins. Follow the directions below to help her get out of this mess!

Directions: Each trophy below is labeled with a division problem. Each trophy plate is labeled with a different quotient. Shade the most reasonable quotient for each problem. Divide to check your estimate. Show your work on another sheet of paper. Then write the correct quotient on the trophy's blank plate.

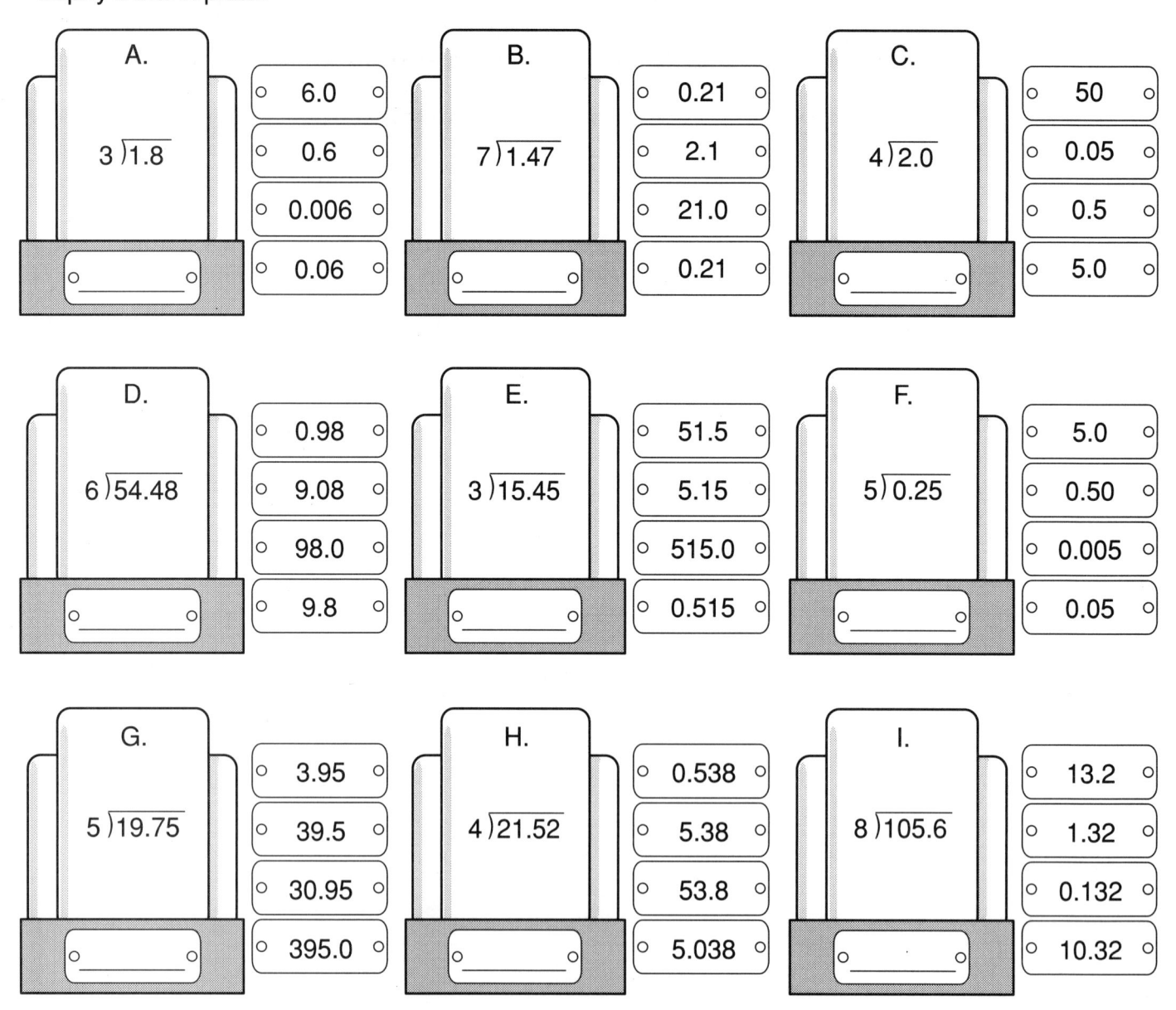

A. $3\overline{)1.8}$
- 6.0
- 0.6
- 0.006
- 0.06

B. $7\overline{)1.47}$
- 0.21
- 2.1
- 21.0
- 0.21

C. $4\overline{)2.0}$
- 50
- 0.05
- 0.5
- 5.0

D. $6\overline{)54.48}$
- 0.98
- 9.08
- 98.0
- 9.8

E. $3\overline{)15.45}$
- 51.5
- 5.15
- 515.0
- 0.515

F. $5\overline{)0.25}$
- 5.0
- 0.50
- 0.005
- 0.05

G. $5\overline{)19.75}$
- 3.95
- 39.5
- 30.95
- 395.0

H. $4\overline{)21.52}$
- 0.538
- 5.38
- 53.8
- 5.038

I. $8\overline{)105.6}$
- 13.2
- 1.32
- 0.132
- 10.32

BRAINWORK: The judges kept one problem in a secret place in case of a tie. It's $4\overline{)0.148}$. Can you solve it?

Name: _____ **Power Skill:** Identifying lines

Coastlines

Complete the activity below to learn more about lines, line segments, and rays. As you read the instructions in the box, look carefully at the picture below. Locate and color each type of line or lines.

Instructions:
1. Color an example of a *line* green.
2. Color 3 examples of a *ray* yellow.
3. Color 3 pairs of *parallel lines* red.
4. Color 3 examples of a *perpendicular line* blue. Circle the corners where the lines intersect at right angles.
5. Color any other 3 *line segments* brown.

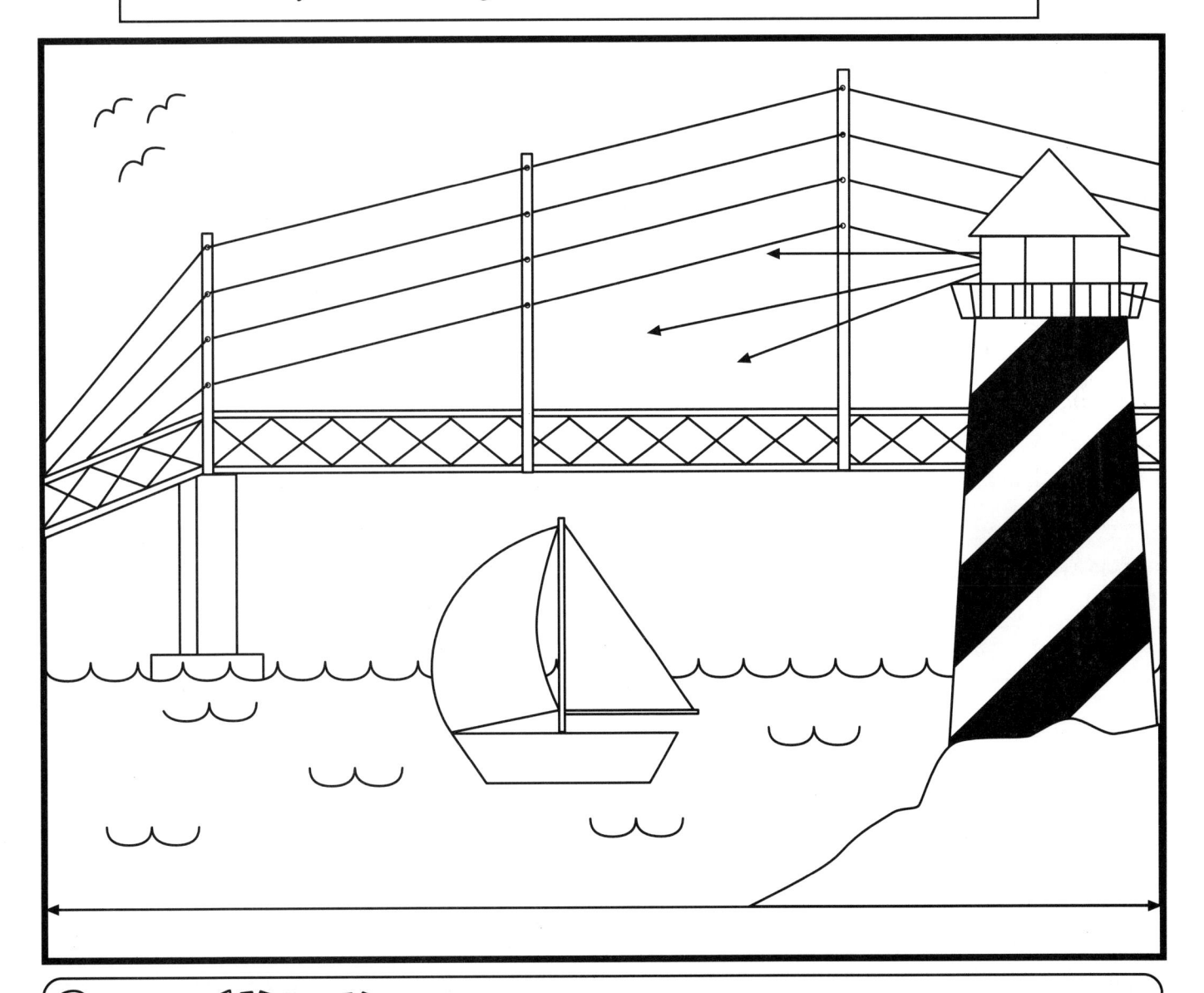

BRAINWORK: On the back of this sheet, write the alphabet in capital block letters. Circle the letters that contain parallel lines. Underline the letters that have perpendicular lines.

©2001 The Education Center, Inc. • *Power Practice • Math* • TEC2667 • Key p. 106

Name: _____ Power Skill: Identifying angles

Angle Construction

If you could remove the front wall of a house, you would find an array of beams and joints designed to give the wall and roof strength. Use a protractor to measure the numbered angles in this house. Next, decide if each is an *acute, right,* or *obtuse* angle. Then write the angle number beside the correct heading.

Acute angles: _____
Right angles: _____
Obtuse angles: _____

BRAINWORK: On the back of this sheet, draw a circular pizza. Divide it into 3 pieces so that the point of 1 piece forms a right angle, the second piece forms an acute angle, and the third piece forms an obtuse angle. Label the pieces.

Name: _____   **Power Skill:** Drawing common polygons

Party at the Polygons'

Once a month, the Polygon family has a special dinner together. Mrs. Polygon uses the unique fine china plates on the shelf below. Help her decide who gets which plate by reading the clues in the box. Next, identify the shape of each plate on the shelf by coloring it as the clues suggest. Then draw the correct dinner plate on the table at each family member's place.

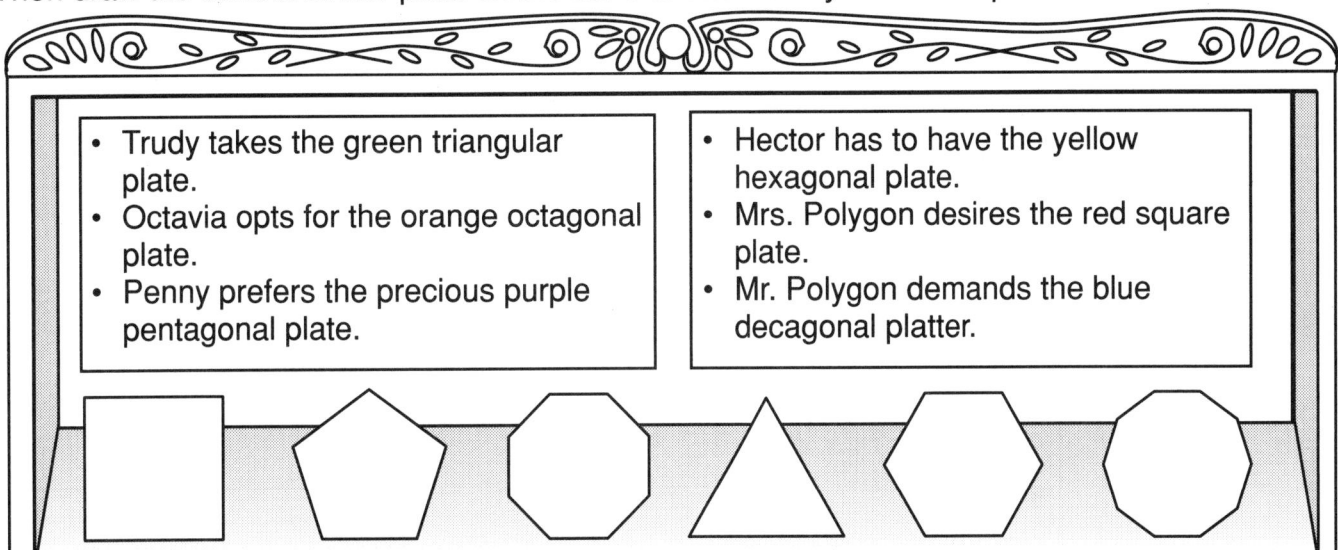

- Trudy takes the green triangular plate.
- Octavia opts for the orange octagonal plate.
- Penny prefers the precious purple pentagonal plate.

- Hector has to have the yellow hexagonal plate.
- Mrs. Polygon desires the red square plate.
- Mr. Polygon demands the blue decagonal platter.

BRAINWORK: Look through old magazines to find pictures of real-life objects that are examples of various polygons. Cut out the pictures and glue them onto construction paper. Label each picture with the name of its shape.

©2001 The Education Center, Inc. • Power Practice • Math • TEC2667 • Key p. 106

Note to the teacher: Provide each student with crayons or colored pencils, magazines, scissors, glue, and construction paper to complete this activity.

Name: _____
Power Skill: Identifying quadrilaterals

Terra Turtle's Fashions

Terra is a fashionable turtle. Use the color code below to color the quadrilaterals on her new "a-quad-ics" bathing suit. Then rearrange the letters found on the trapezoids to find out what kind of bathing suit Terra Turtle bought.

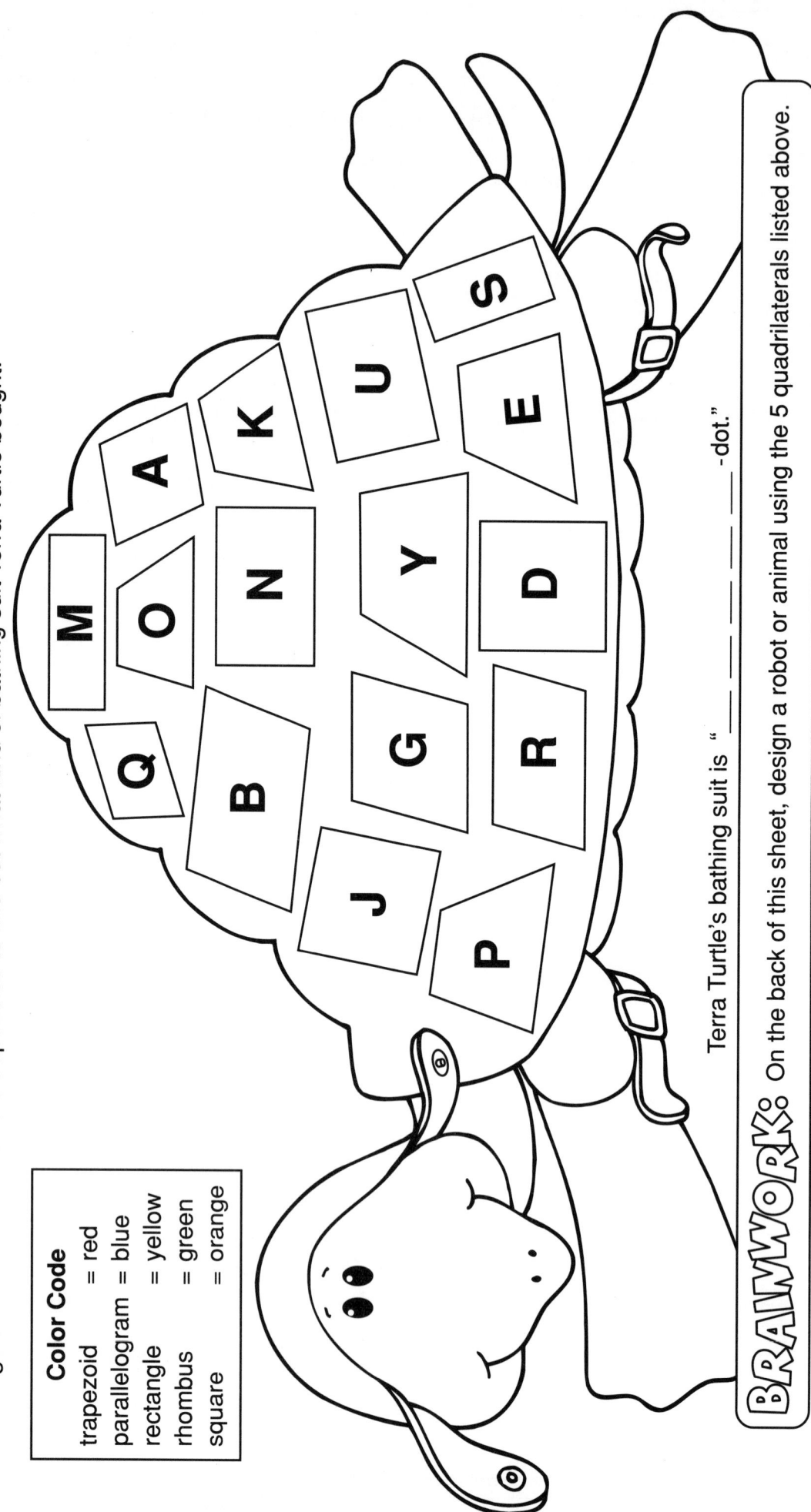

Color Code
trapezoid = red
parallelogram = blue
rectangle = yellow
rhombus = green
square = orange

Terra Turtle's bathing suit is " __ __ __ __ __ -dot."

BRAINWORK: On the back of this sheet, design a robot or animal using the 5 quadrilaterals listed above.

Note to the teacher: Provide each student with crayons or colored pencils to complete this activity.

36 ©2001 The Education Center, Inc. • Power Practice • Math • TEC2667 • Key p. 106

Name: _____   **Power Skill:** Classifying triangles

Try a Tasty Triangle

The Polygon Bakery specializes in geometric cookies. Tuesday is Triangular Cookie Day. Your job is to decorate these special triangular cookies according to the instructions of the head baker shown below.

- Decorate the *right*-triangle cookies with light blue frosting and rainbow sprinkles.
- Decorate the *isosceles*-triangle cookies to look like pieces of pizza.
- Decorate the *equilateral*-triangle cookies to look like wedges of Swiss cheese.
- Decorate the *scalene*-triangle cookies with green frosting and blue candy pieces.

BRAINWORK: Choose 1 kind of triangular cookie from above. On the back of this sheet, draw a picture to show the best way to pack this type in a round box. How many will fit in 1 layer?

©2001 The Education Center, Inc. • *Power Practice* • Math • TEC2667 • Key p. 107

Note to the teacher: Provide students with crayons or colored pencils to complete this activity.

37

Name: _____   **Power Skill:** Identifying geometric solids

Hats Off to Our Presidents

While he listened to his teacher talk about geometric solids, Patrick looked up at a portrait of President Lincoln wearing his famous stovepipe hat. "I wonder," thought Patrick, "what President Lincoln would look like if his hat were shaped like a geometric solid other than a cylinder."

Identify the geometric-solid shape of each of the hats Patrick imagined for President Lincoln. Write your answers on the lines below. Then design hats for the other 6 presidents using the geometric shapes below their portraits.

George Washington — **cone**

Thomas Jefferson — **sphere**

John F. Kennedy — **cylinder**

Ronald W. Reagan — **rectangular solid**

George H. W. Bush — **pyramid**

George W. Bush — **cube**

1. _____
2. _____
3. _____
4. _____
5. _____
6. _____

BRAINWORK: On the back of this sheet, design a geometric-solid hat using recyclable materials.

Name: _____   Power Skill: Similar and congruent polygons

Polygon Python

Why is a python so difficult to trick? Find out by studying the polygons on the python's back to find similar and congruent shapes.

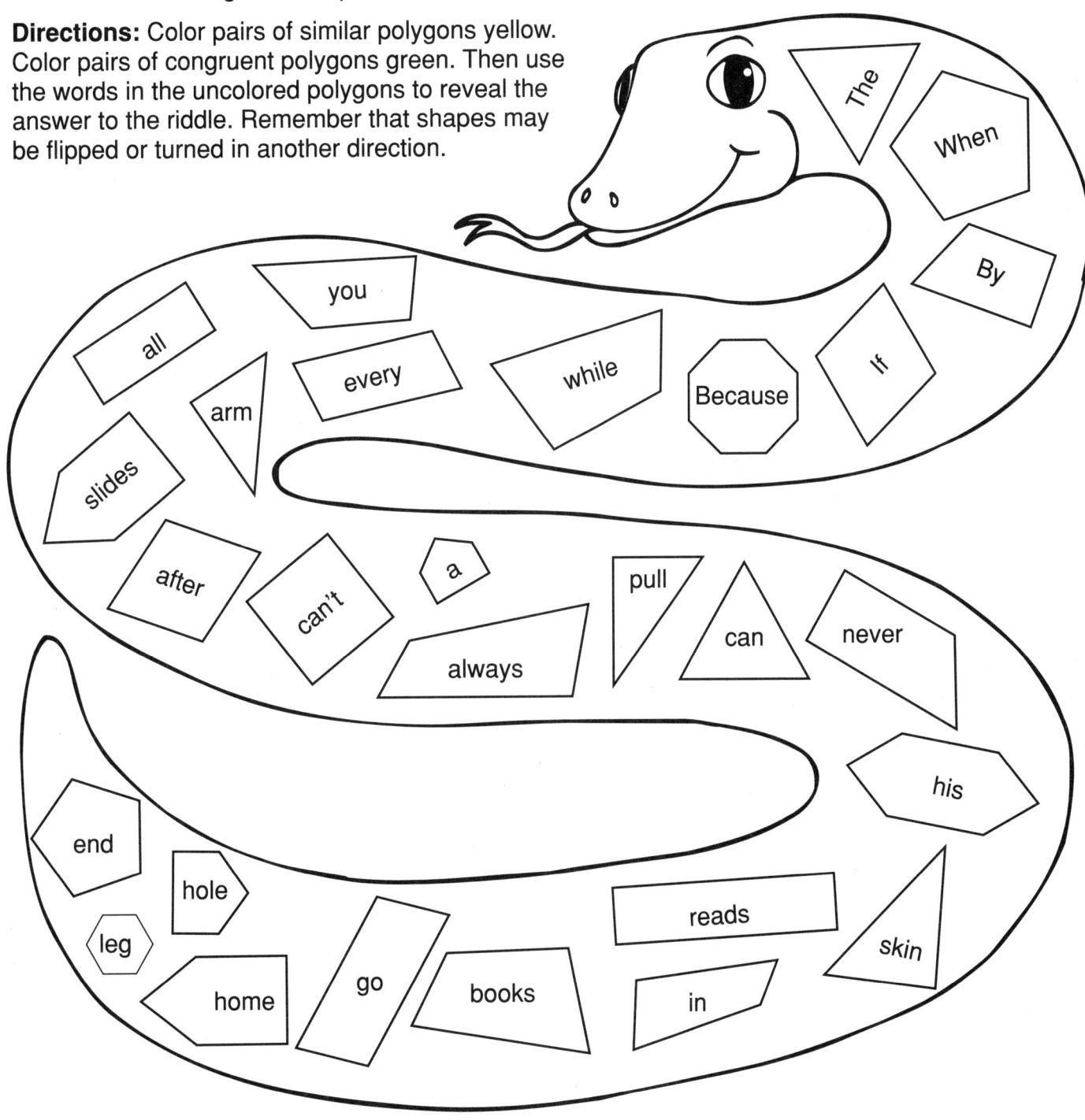

Directions: Color pairs of similar polygons yellow. Color pairs of congruent polygons green. Then use the words in the uncolored polygons to reveal the answer to the riddle. Remember that shapes may be flipped or turned in another direction.

Why is a python so difficult to trick? _____

BRAINWORK: On the back of this sheet, use a ruler to draw a rectangle. Then draw a similar rectangle with sides that are twice as long.

Name: _____   **Power Skill:** Similar and congruent polygons

Patches of Patterned Polygons

As you produce pretty patches of patterned polygons below, remember that *congruent figures* have the same size and shape. *Similar figures* have the same shape but not necessarily the same size.

A.

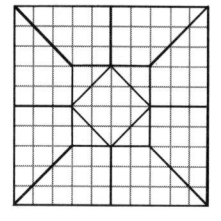

Quigley can quilt congruent corners quickly, but he needs your help. Use a ruler to draw a pattern patch congruent to patch A in the grid square A-1. Then draw a pattern patch congruent to patch B in the grid square B-1.

B.

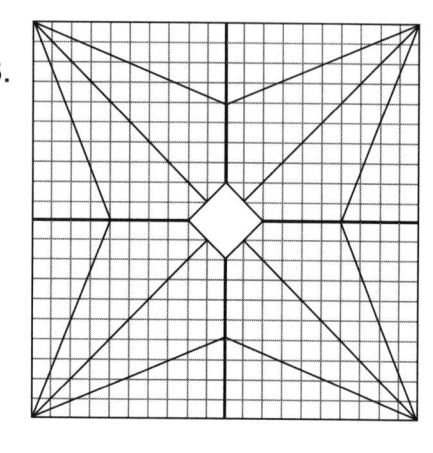

A-1.

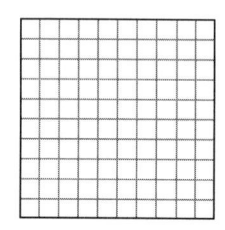

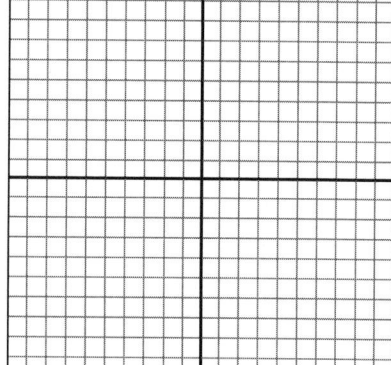

Simpson sews similar seams on silky satin. Can you help him draw the designs?

B-1.

First, draw a similar pattern patch twice as large as patch A in the grid square A-2.

Then draw a similar block that is half the size of patch B in the grid square B-2.

A-2.

B-2.

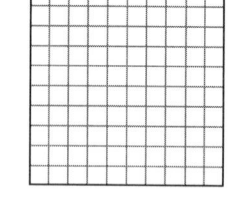

BRAINWORK: Choose 3 colors for coloring pattern patches A and A-1. Choose 3 different colors for coloring B and B-1. Within those pattern blocks, color the congruent shapes the same color. Use lighter or darker shades of the same colors to show the similiar shapes in A-2 and B-2.

40   ©2001 The Education Center, Inc. • Power Practice • Math • TEC2667

Name: _____ **Power Skill:** Identifying symmetry

Sensational Symmetry

Picture yourself folding a paper heart or 5-point star in half. The halves of each of these shapes match exactly. The fold creates a *line of symmetry,* and the 2 resulting equal parts are described as *symmetrical.* Follow the directions below to complete each section on symmetry.

A. Each figure below has only 1 line of symmetry. Draw the line for each figure in the appropriate place.

1. ♥ 
2. ♠ 
3. M
4. ◠ 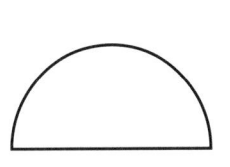
5. ↑

B. Some figures have more than 1 line of symmetry. Draw the lines of symmetry on each figure below. Then tell how many lines of symmetry each one has.

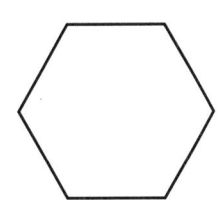

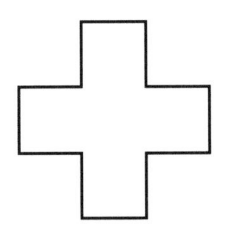

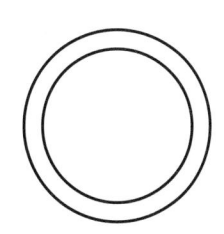

6. (quatrefoil) _____
7. (hexagon) _____
8. (double arrow) _____
9. (plus/cross) _____
10. (circle) _____
11. (rhombus) _____

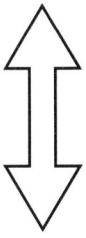

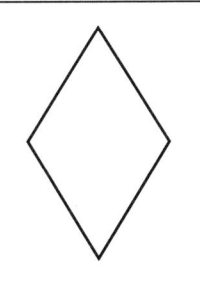

C. Draw the other half of each figure below to show that the figure has line symmetry.

12. 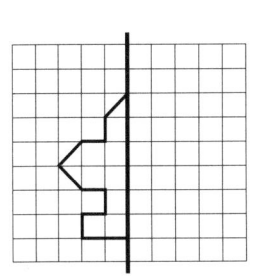
13. 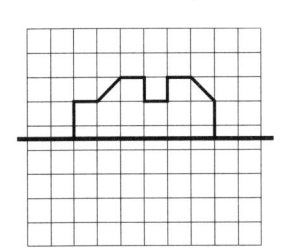
14.

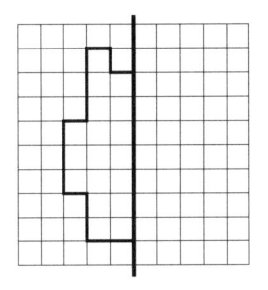

BRAINWORK: Many items in nature are symmetrical. On the back of your paper, list 10 objects that you might see outside. Circle all of the items that are symmetrical.

©2001 The Education Center, Inc. • *Power Practice* • *Math* • TEC2667 • Key p. 107

41

Name: _____   Power Skill: Translations, rotations, and reflections

Transformation Creations

Transformations are made by moving geometric figures in different ways.

Slide a figure to make a *translation*.

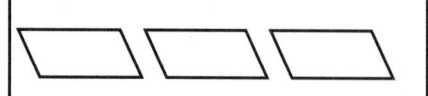

Flip a figure over an imaginary line to make a *reflection*.

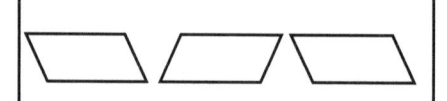

Turn a figure around a point or vertex to make a *rotation*.

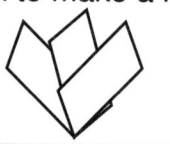

Part I: Study each figure below. Tell if it was created as a translation, reflection, or rotation. Then use the word box to give each creation an appropriate name.

Word Box
Flip-o-saur   Turn-a-lily   Slide-a-mid   Slide-a-pillar   Flip-a-figure   Turn-a-ball

1.

2.

3.

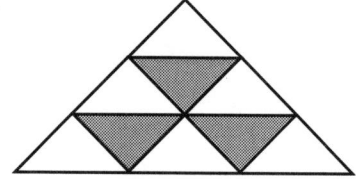

_____
_____

4.

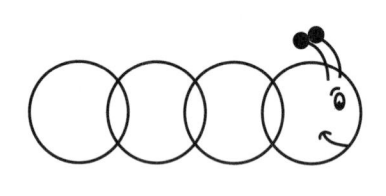

5.

6.

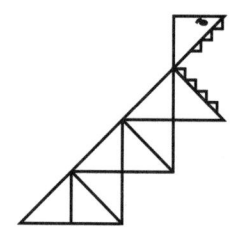

_____
_____

Part II: On the back of this sheet, create a translation, reflection, or rotation figure for each of the following shapes.

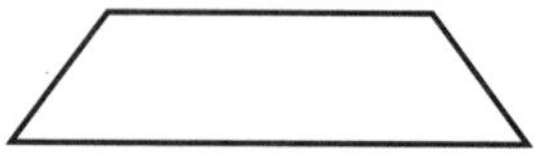

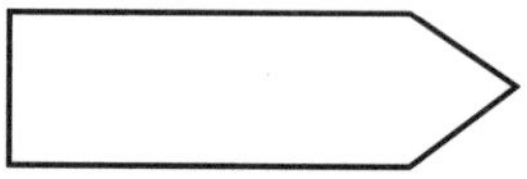

BRAINWORK: Cut a triangle, a half circle, and a rectangle from a sheet of construction paper. Use each shape to create a transformation figure. Then ask a friend to help you name your creations.

Name: _____ **Power Skill:** Locating points on a grid

Shooting for the Stars

Directions: Write the corresponding letter for each ordered pair on the line provided. Then read the completed paragraph to learn more about a great American who aimed for the stars—and made it!

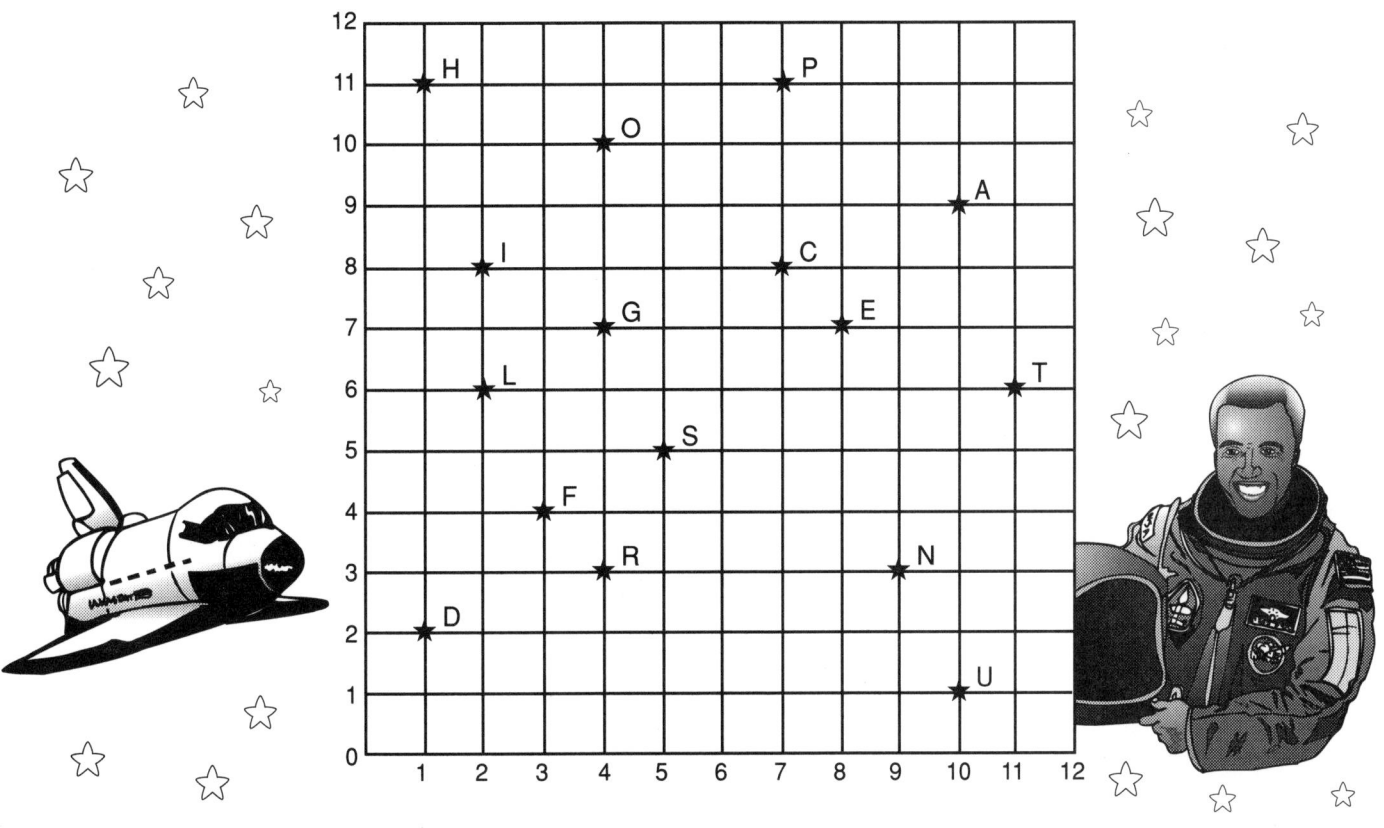

Grid points:
- H (1, 11)
- P (7, 11)
- O (4, 10)
- A (10, 9)
- I (2, 8)
- C (7, 8)
- G (4, 7)
- E (8, 7)
- L (2, 6)
- T (11, 6)
- S (5, 5)
- F (3, 4)
- R (4, 3)
- N (9, 3)
- D (1, 2)
- U (10, 1)

As a little boy, ___ ___ ___ ___ ___ Stewart Bluford Jr. liked to play with model airplanes. He
      (4, 7)(10, 1)(2, 8)(4, 10)(9, 3)

decided he wanted to be an aerospace engineer. His high school guidance counselor told him

that his ___ ___ ___ ___ ___ ___ weren't high enough to attend college. He proved his guidance
   (4, 7)(4, 3)(10, 9)(1, 2)(8, 7)(5, 5)

counselor wrong, graduating from Penn State University. He then ___ ___ ___ ___ ___ ___ ___
                                                                        (11, 6)(4, 3)(10, 9)(2, 8)(9, 3)(8, 7)(1, 2)

as an Air Force pilot and flew missions over Vietnam. After the war, he earned a master's

degree in ___ ___ ___ ___ ___ ___ ___ ___ ___ engineering and began to test and design
         (10, 9)(8, 7)(4, 3)(4, 10)(5, 5)(7, 11)(10, 9)(7, 8)(8, 7)

___ ___ ___ ___ ___ ___ ___ ___. At age 35, he ___ ___ ___ ___ ___ ___ his Ph.D. and applied
(10, 9)(2, 8)(4, 3)(7, 8)(4, 3)(10, 9)(3, 4)(11,6)   (8, 7)(10, 9)(4, 3)(9, 3)(8, 7)(1, 2)

to the NASA ___ ___ ___ ___ ___ ___ ___ ___ ___ Training Program. He completed his training,
              (10, 9)(5, 5)(11, 6)(4, 3)(4, 10)(9, 3)(10, 9)(10, 1)(11, 6)

and, on August 30, 1983, Lieutenant Colonel Bluford became the first Black American to fly in

___ ___ ___ ___ ___!
(5, 5)(7, 11)(10, 9)(7, 8)(8, 7)

BRAINWORK: Write the corresponding letter for each ordered pair to find out the name of the space shuttle that took Lieutenant Colonel Bluford into space.

___ ___ ___ ___ ___ ___ ___ ___ ___
(7, 8)(1, 11)(10, 9)(2, 6)(2, 6)(8, 7)(9, 3)(4, 7)(8, 7)(4, 3)

Name: _____ Power Skill: Graphing ordered pairs

What's Your Sign?

Ordered pairs represent locations on a grid. Plot and connect the following points in order on the grid below. Then use a different colored pencil to shade each sign.

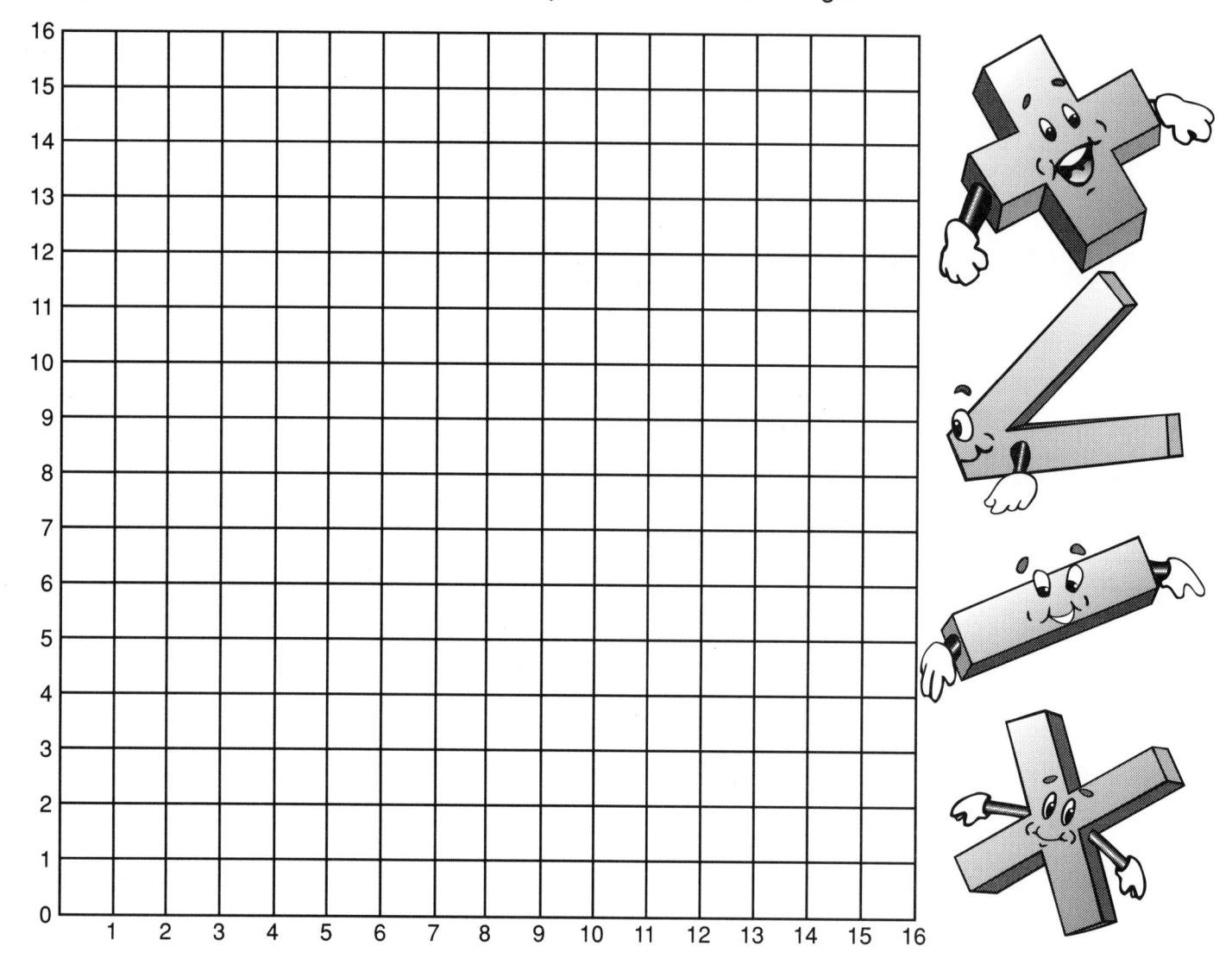

1. (0, 2), (0, 4), (2, 4), (2, 6), (4, 6), (4, 4), (6, 4), (6, 2), (4, 2), (4, 0), (2, 0), (2, 2), (0, 2)

2. (8, 1), (10, 3), (8, 5), (9, 6), (11, 4), (13, 6), (14, 5), (12, 3), (14, 1), (13, 0), (11, 2), (9, 0), (8, 1)

3. (6, 10), (0, 13), (6, 16), (6, 15), (2, 13), (6, 11), (6, 10)

4. (10, 10), (16, 13), (10, 16), (10, 15), (14, 13), (10, 11), (10, 10)

BRAINWORK: On the back of this sheet, write 6 problems using the math signs you graphed. Have a classmate answer the problems.

©2001 The Education Center, Inc. • Power Practice • Math • TEC2667 • Key p. 107

44   Note to the teacher: Students will need colored pencils to complete this activity.

Name: _____   **Power Skill:** Coordinate graphing

As "Easel" As 1-2-3!

Try your hand at designing a picture that can be formed by connecting points on a grid.

Create each picture by marking 20 different points on each grid below. Record the coordinate pairs for each point in the spaces provided next to the grid. Be sure to list the coordinate pairs in the order in which they should be connected. Then connect the dots to reveal your pictures.

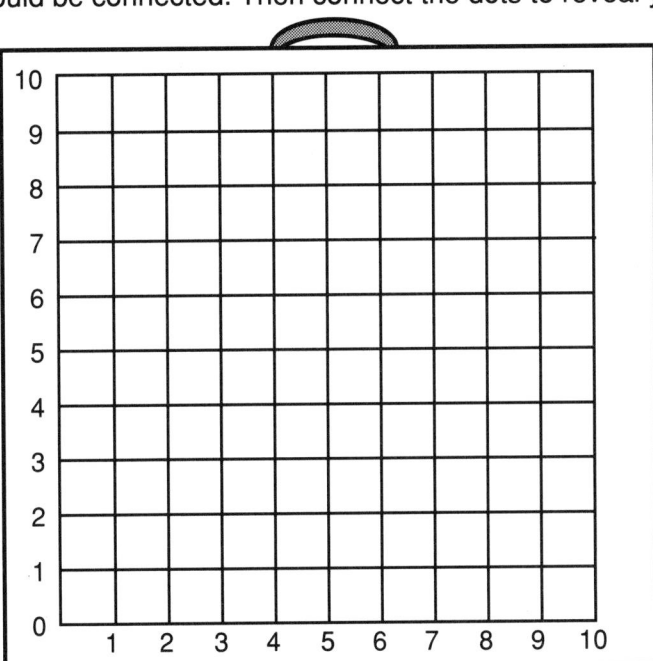

PICTURE 1

Picture 1: Coordinate Pairs

1. _____   11. _____
2. _____   12. _____
3. _____   13. _____
4. _____   14. _____
5. _____   15. _____
6. _____   16. _____
7. _____   17. _____
8. _____   18. _____
9. _____   19. _____
10. _____   20. _____

Picture 2: Coordinate Pairs

1. _____   11. _____
2. _____   12. _____
3. _____   13. _____
4. _____   14. _____
5. _____   15. _____
6. _____   16. _____
7. _____   17. _____
8. _____   18. _____
9. _____   19. _____
10. _____   20. _____

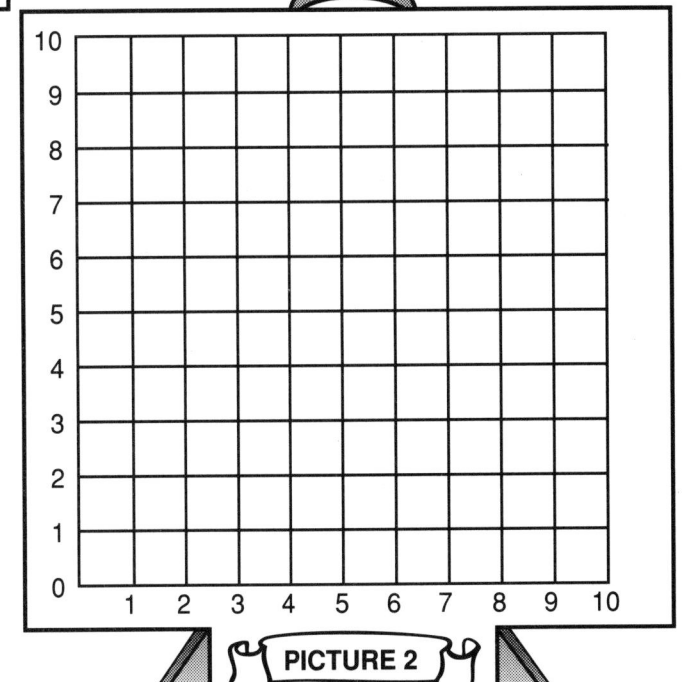

PICTURE 2

BRAINWORK: Rewrite each pair of coordinates on another sheet of paper. Then have a friend re-create your drawing by using your coordinates and a blank sheet of graph paper.

©2001 The Education Center, Inc. • Power Practice • Math • TEC2667

Name: _____

Power Skill: Constructing circles

Circle Art

After learning how to construct circles in math class, Cedric spent an evening using his compass to create circle pictures. He followed these steps to make the circle(s) for each picture:

- Draw a point. This is the center of the circle.

- Start at the point. Use a ruler to draw a line the length of your radius.

- Place the point of the compass on the center point. Place the pencil point on the other end of the radius.

- Hold the compass point still. Turn the compass around on the point to make a circle.

- Erase the radius line. Add details to the circle.

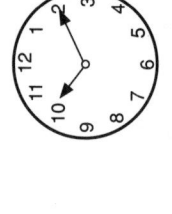

Directions: In the space below, create each of the circle pictures described in the list. Use a metric ruler and a compass to draw accurate circles. Then use crayons or colored pencils to add details to your drawings. Use the back of this page if you need more room.

1. ladybug—1 cm radius
2. button—10 mm radius
3. lollipop—15 mm radius
4. bagel—25 mm radius
5. triple-scoop ice-cream cone—5 mm radius each
6. lemon slice—2 cm radius
7. 3 soap bubbles—1 cm radius each
8. 2 chocolate chip cookies—5 mm radius each
9. world map—2 cm radius

BRAINWORK: Cedric also learned how to calculate *circumference*, or distance around a circle, by using the following formula: $\pi = 3.14$, $C = 2\pi \times r$. Use this formula and a calculator to find the circumference for each circle you drew. Write each answer below its corresponding drawing.

Note to the teacher: Provide each student with 1 copy of this page, a compass, a ruler, and colored pencils. If desired, provide calculators for students to complete the Brainwork problem.

©2001 The Education Center, Inc. • *Power Practice* • *Math* • TEC2667 • Key p. 107

Name: _____ **Power Skill:** Using customary measurement

Optical Illusions

Have you ever been tricked by an optical illusion? Using a ruler marked in 16th inches and a sharpened pencil, follow the directions below to create an optical illusion to share with a friend.

Directions:

A. Draw a line $\frac{13}{16}$" to the right, then $1\frac{1}{8}$" up.

B. Draw a line $\frac{7}{8}$" to the right, then $1\frac{1}{8}$" up, then $2\frac{3}{16}$" to the right.

C. Draw a line $\frac{15}{16}$" to the right, then $1\frac{1}{8}$" up, then $2\frac{1}{8}$" to the right.

D. Draw a line 1" to the right, then $1\frac{1}{8}$" up, then $2\frac{1}{16}$" to the right.

E. Draw a line $1\frac{1}{16}$" to the right, then $1\frac{1}{8}$" up, then 2" to the right.

F. Draw a line $1\frac{1}{8}$" to the right, then $1\frac{1}{8}$" up, then $1\frac{15}{16}$" to the right.

G. Draw a line $1\frac{3}{16}$" to the right, then $1\frac{1}{8}$" up, then $1\frac{7}{8}$" to the right.

H. Draw a line $1\frac{1}{4}$" to the right, then $1\frac{1}{8}$" up, then $1\frac{13}{16}$" to the right.

I. Draw a line $1\frac{5}{16}$" to the right, then $1\frac{1}{8}$" up, then $1\frac{3}{4}$" to the right.

J. Draw a line $1\frac{3}{8}$" to the right, then $1\frac{1}{8}$" up, then $1\frac{11}{16}$" to the right.

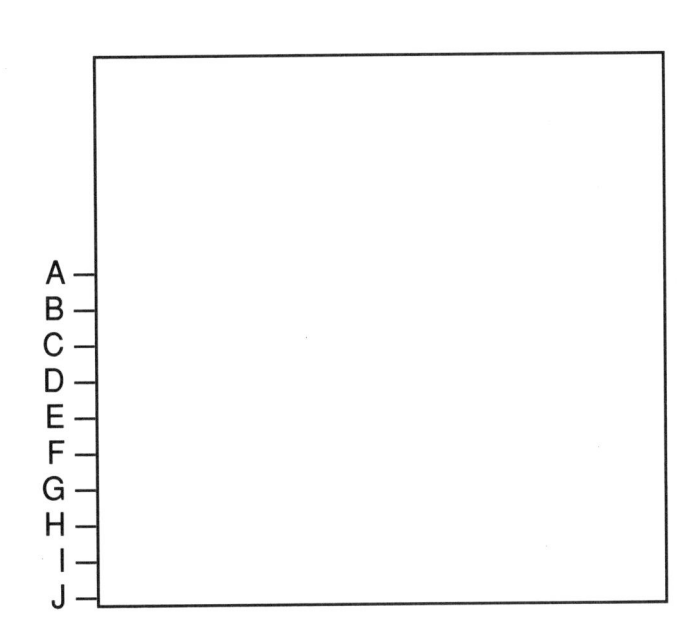

Hold the paper at arm's length. Which side appears higher: the right side or the left side? Why? _____

_____

_____

BRAINWORK: Look at the 2 lines below. Which line looks longer? Measure the lines. Why do you think 1 line looks longer than the other?

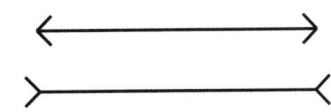

©2001 The Education Center, Inc. • *Power Practice • Math •* TEC2667 • Key p. 107

Note to the teacher: Students will need a ruler marked in 16th inches and a sharpened pencil.

Name: _____ **Power Skill:** Using customary measurement

Robo-Specs

Congratulations! You have just been named the winner of the Raving Robot Company's national contest for designing the best new miniature robot. The company loves your design, but they need the exact measurements before they can start production.

Directions: Write the correct measurements for each part of your robot listed below. Measure to the nearest fraction of an inch as indicated in each section. Reduce your answers to the lowest terms.

Measure to the nearest $\frac{1}{2}$".
1. Height of the robot from top to bottom _____
2. Width of the robot from elbow to elbow _____

Measure to the nearest $\frac{1}{4}$".
3. Length of the robot's legs, from bottom of hip to top of circle _____
4. Width of the robot's shoulders, including both circles _____
5. Width of the robot's hips _____

Measure to the nearest $\frac{1}{8}$".
6. Width of the robot's waist _____
7. Width of the robot's head _____
8. Width of the top of the robot's small chest triangle _____
9. Length inside the robot's upper arm, from armpit to elbow _____
10. Diameter of the robot's shoulder circle _____

Measure to the nearest $\frac{1}{16}$".
11. Width of the robot's legs _____
12. Width of the robot's hat _____
13. Width of the robot's neck _____
14. Diameter of the robot's foot circle _____
15. Diameter of the robot's nose circle _____

BRAINWORK: Draw your own robot on the back of this sheet. Include lines that measure 2", $1\frac{3}{4}$", and $1\frac{1}{8}$". Also use circles with diameters of $\frac{1}{2}$", $\frac{1}{4}$", and $\frac{3}{16}$" along with other shapes. Give your drawing to a classmate and see if he or she can find the lines and circles with these measurements.

Name: _____   Power Skill: Using metric measurement

Going Buggy!

Dr. Millie Pede, a renowned entomologist, is measuring her collection of centipedes and millipedes. Help her by following the directions below.

Directions: Measure each centipede to the nearest centimeter and each millipede to the nearest millimeter. Then identify which centipedes and millipedes are the same length. Color each matching pair a different color.

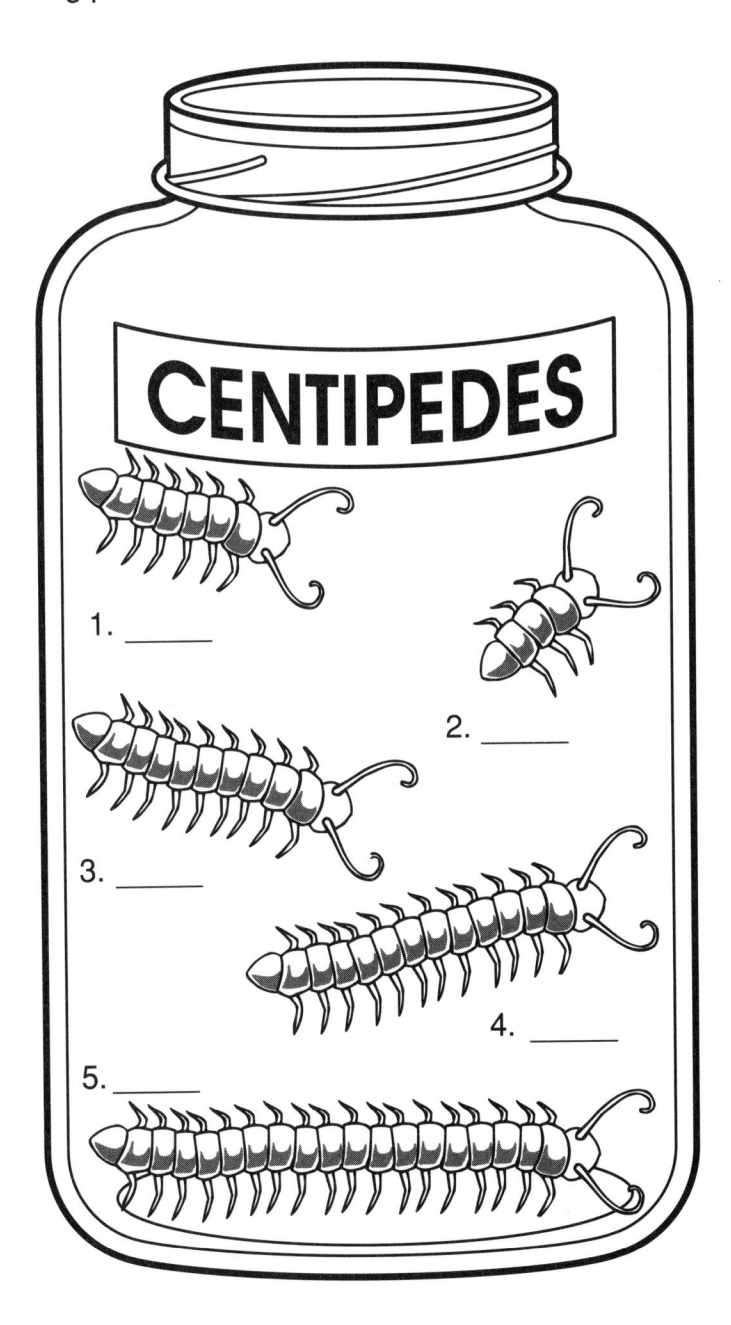

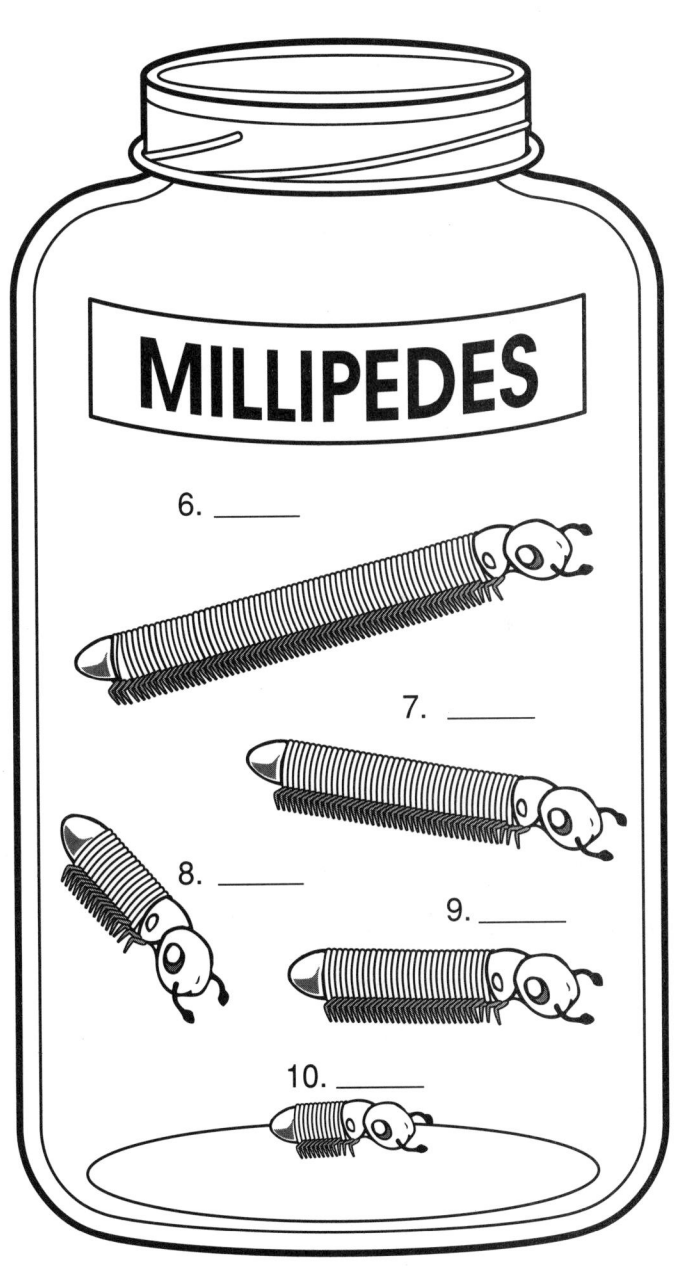

CENTIPEDES

1. _____
2. _____
3. _____
4. _____
5. _____

MILLIPEDES

6. _____
7. _____
8. _____
9. _____
10. _____

BRAINWORK: Add the lengths of all the millipedes together. Write your answer in millimeters and centimeters. Then add the lengths of all the centipedes together. Write your answer in centimeters and millimeters.

©2001 The Education Center, Inc. • Power Practice • Math • TEC2667 • Key p. 108

49

Name: _____ **Power Skill:** Understanding metric measurement

Sizin' Up the Family Farm

Farmer Gram has decided that she wants to make her farm part of the global market, so she's decided to measure everything on her farm using the metric system. Help Farmer Gram by circling the most reasonable unit of measure she should use to measure each item below.

1. length of the fence
   m   cm   km

2. height of the barn
   km   m   mm

3. amount of water in the pond
   kl   l   ml

4. mass of a chick
   mg   hg   g

5. amount of milk produced by the cow each day
   l   dl   kl

6. mass of the tractor
   kg   dg   g

7. height of the silo
   km   dm   m

8. amount of water in the trough
   ml   l   dal

9. mass of a bale of hay
   g   hg   mg

10. length of a chicken feather
    cm   m   hm

11. amount of rainwater in the rain gauge
    kl   l   cl

12. mass of a kernel of corn
    mg   hg   g

13. mass of the pig
    g   kg   dg

14. distance between the hens
    dam   m   hm

BRAINWORK: Think about your classroom as part of the global market. List 5 things you could measure in length, 5 things in volume, and 5 things in mass. Next to each, write the most reasonable unit of measurement you would use to measure each item.

Name: _____ Power Skill: Understanding customary measurement

Draco's Dream Dinner

Draco has been thinking about his dream dinner for days and days. Unfortunately, he has gotten the measurements all mixed up. Figure out how much food and drink he hopes to get by reading the chart below and then following each set of directions.

Abbreviations

ounce = oz.   pint = pt.
pound = lb.   quart = qt.
ton = T   gallon = gal.
cup = c.

Equivalents

16 oz. = 1 lb.   2 pt. = 1 qt.
2,000 lb. = 1 T   4 qt. = 1 gal.
2 c. = 1 pt.

A. Look at each dinner treat below. Circle the best estimate for each treat's weight.

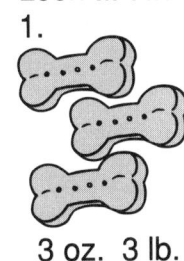

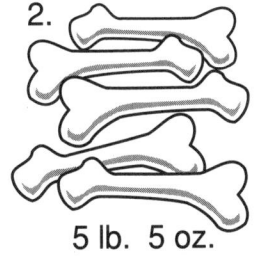

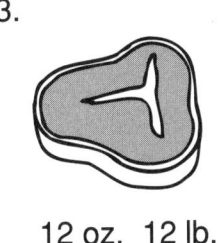

1. 3 oz.   3 lb.
2. 5 lb.   5 oz.
3. 12 oz. 12 lb.
4. 55 oz. 55 lb.
5. 300 lb. 3 T

B. Look carefully at the measurement markings on the containers below. Shade in each container to show the amount of water Draco is dreaming of listed below the container. Then circle all containers that show an equal amount.

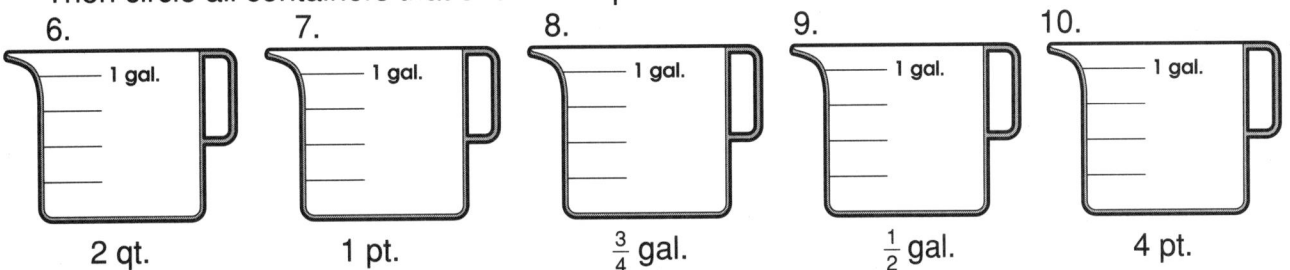

6. 2 qt.
7. 1 pt.
8. $\frac{3}{4}$ gal.
9. $\frac{1}{2}$ gal.
10. 4 pt.

C. Look at the level of water Draco is dreaming about in each container. Circle the measurement that indicates the amount of water in each container. There may be more than 1 correct answer for each.

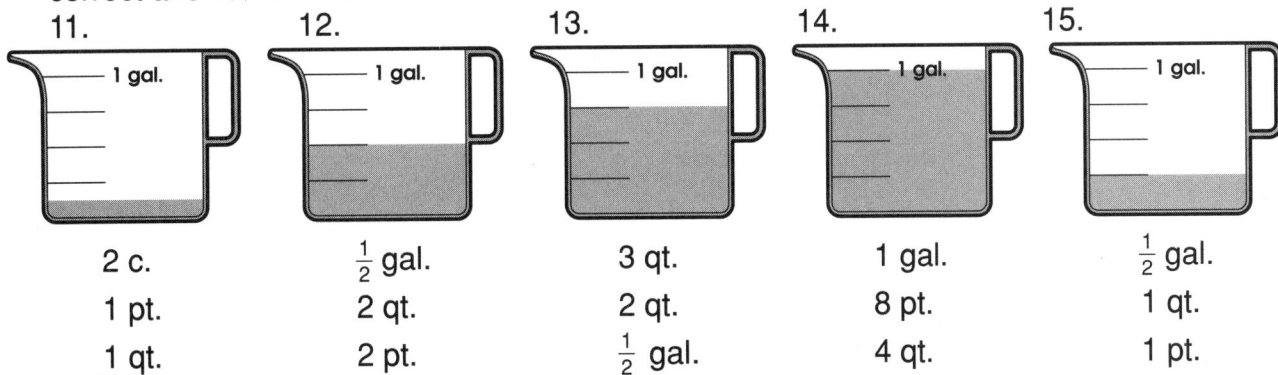

11. 2 c.
    1 pt.
    1 qt.

12. $\frac{1}{2}$ gal.
    2 qt.
    2 pt.

13. 3 qt.
    2 qt.
    $\frac{1}{2}$ gal.

14. 1 gal.
    8 pt.
    4 qt.

15. $\frac{1}{2}$ gal.
    1 qt.
    1 pt.

BRAINWORK: On the back of this sheet, write a paragraph about Draco's dream dinner. Then illustrate your story, including several of the items above.

Name: _____ Power Skill: Understanding Fahrenheit temperature

All-Weather Wardrobe

Billy Bluejeans wants to plan his wardrobe in advance for the occasions listed below. Follow the directions to help Billy choose the appropriate clothing.

Directions: Use the thermometer to help you decide which temperature is the most reasonable for each situation listed below. Lightly color in the correct answer.

1. Playing flag football in the fall — 50°F / 80°F

2. Building the best snowman with his buddies — 30°F / 75°F

3. Swimming in the surf during summer vacation — 40°F / 86°F

4. Raking the rust-colored leaves that have fallen to the ground — 20°F / 62°F

5. Planting a vegetable patch with his pals — 73°F / 95°F

6. Water-skiing on the warm Florida waters — 56°F / 82°F

7. Picking vine-ripened vegetables from his garden — 37°F / 78°F

8. Snowboarding the snow-covered slopes with his sisters — 29°F / 55°F

9. Walking beneath the willow trees on a wintry day — 0°F / 35°F

10. Riding a horse past the historic flower gardens — 45°F / 73°F

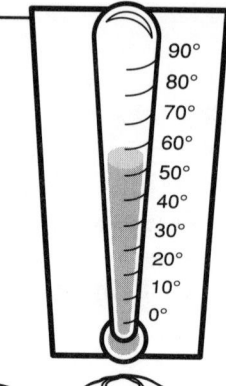

BRAINWORK: On the back of this page, write about an occasion when you had to decide between cold-weather clothes and warm-weather clothes. Include the temperature and what clothes you selected.

Name: _____   **Power Skill:** Celsius and Fahrenheit temperature

Taking the Temperature Tour

Maxie, a million-dollar movie star, is off on a monthlong tour to promote her latest film. She will be visiting 10 European cities. Maxie has checked the weather forecast for those cities, but they measure temperature in degrees Celsius instead of degrees Fahrenheit, so she can't tell what the temperatures will be like. Follow the directions below to help Maxie convert each temperature from degrees Celsius to degrees Fahrenheit.

Directions: Convert degrees Celsius to degrees Fahrenheit by multiplying the temperature in the Celsius column by 1.8 and adding 32. Then round your answer to the nearest degree and record it in the Fahrenheit column.

City	Celsius Temperature	Fahrenheit Temperature	City	Celsius Temperature	Fahrenheit Temperature
London	4°C		Madrid	9°C	
Paris	15°C		Oslo	0°C	
Athens	10°C		Berlin	18°C	
Zurich	22°C		Lisbon	12°C	
Rome	13°C		Dublin	7°C	

1. What is the difference between London and Paris in degrees Celsius? _____ In degrees Fahrenheit? _____

2. What is the difference between Madrid and Lisbon in degrees Celsius? _____ In degrees Fahrenheit? _____

3. How much warmer is Athens than Oslo in degrees Celsius? _____ In degrees Fahrenheit? _____

4. How much colder is Rome than Berlin in degrees Celsius? _____ In degrees Fahrenheit? _____

5. Which is warmer: 13°C or 45°F? _____

6. Which is colder: 21°F or 3°C? _____

BRAINWORK: Find out today's high and low temperatures in degrees Fahrenheit in your town and convert them to degrees Celsius.

Name: _____   Power Skill: Determining elapsed time

Amazing Mouse Maze

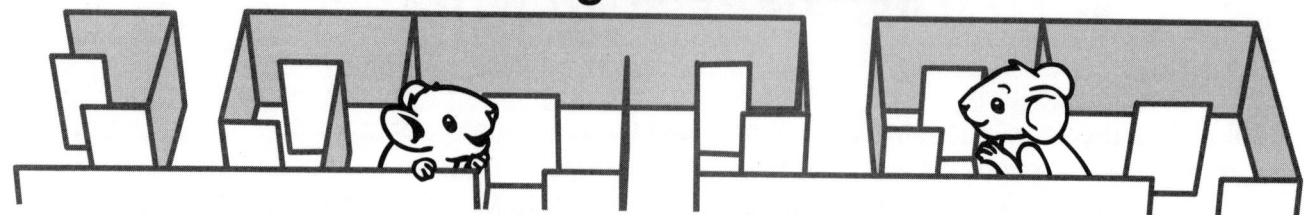

The Amazing Mouse Maze competition has just been completed. The judge needs your help to find the winner. First, figure out the elapsed time of each contestant listed below and record it in the corresponding column. Then determine the placement of each contestant from 1st through 10th and record it in the last column.

Contestant	Start Time	Finish Time	Elapsed Time	Place
1. Milly Mouse	3:45	4:41		
2. Marty Mouse	3:53	4:53		
3. Melvin Mouse	4:01	4:54		
4. Misty Mouse	4:12	5:25		
5. Monica Mouse	4:21	5:10		
6. Melanie Mouse	4:31	5:52		
7. Martin Mouse	4:42	5:29		
8. Mitch Mouse	4:54	6:02		
9. Meredith Mouse	5:05	6:21		
10. Maurice Mouse	5:15	6:37		

11. What is the elapsed time between the time Milly Mouse begins and Maurice Mouse finishes? _____

12. What is the elapsed time between the time the 1st place mouse begins and the 10th place mouse finishes? _____

BRAINWORK: List the times you get up in the morning, go to school, get home, and go to bed. What is the elapsed time between the time you wake up and the time you go to school? The time you get home? The time you go to bed?

Name: _____   Power Skill: Finding area

Tools of the Trade

When it comes to landscaping flower gardens, Green Gables Garden Company is an expert. The company *does* use rakes, shovels, and trowels to do its work, but the sign on the fence lists its *real* tools of the trade! Use the formulas to find the areas of the gardens below. Then write each area in the corresponding shape. The first one has been done for you.

1. Annie Alyssum's garden

   50 ft.²   length = 10 ft.
             width = 5 ft.

2. Belinda Buttercup's garden

   base = 3 m
   height = 6 m

3. Gertrude Gardenia's garden

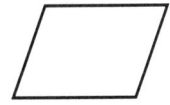

   base = 300 cm
   height = 400 cm

4. Francine Freesia's garden

   length = 6 m
   width = 4 m

5. Irene Iris's garden

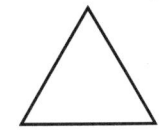

   base = 3 ft.
   height = 3 ft.

6. Terri Tulip's garden

   length = 6 ft.
   width = 2 ft.

7. Chris Chrysanthemum's garden

   base = 7 ft.
   height = 2 ft.

8. Hannah Heather's garden

   length = 7 m
   width = 3 m

9. Lila Lavender's garden

   base = 3.2 m
   height = 6.4 m

10. Druscilla Dahlia's garden

    length = 4 ft.
    width = 8 ft.

11. Carrie Carnation's garden

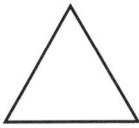

    base = 400 cm
    height = 400 cm

12. Patricia Petunia's garden

    length = 2,100 cm
    width = 700 cm

Green Gables Garden Company's Tools of the Trade

▭ length x width
▱ base x height
△ ½ base x height

BRAINWORK: Whose garden is larger: Hannah Heather's or Carrie Carnation's?
Hint: 100 cm = 1 m. Show your answer by shading in the garden's shape.

©2001 The Education Center, Inc. • Power Practice • Math • TEC2667 • Key p. 108   55

Name: _____   Power Skill: Area of irregular figures

WANTED: Spacious Places

Bowzer, Buddy, and Boomer are pooches that have outgrown their current exercise areas. Look below at the layouts their owners are considering.

Directions: Estimate the area of each layout. Write your estimate on the line provided. Then write the letter of the layout that provides each dog with the most running room on the corresponding animal.

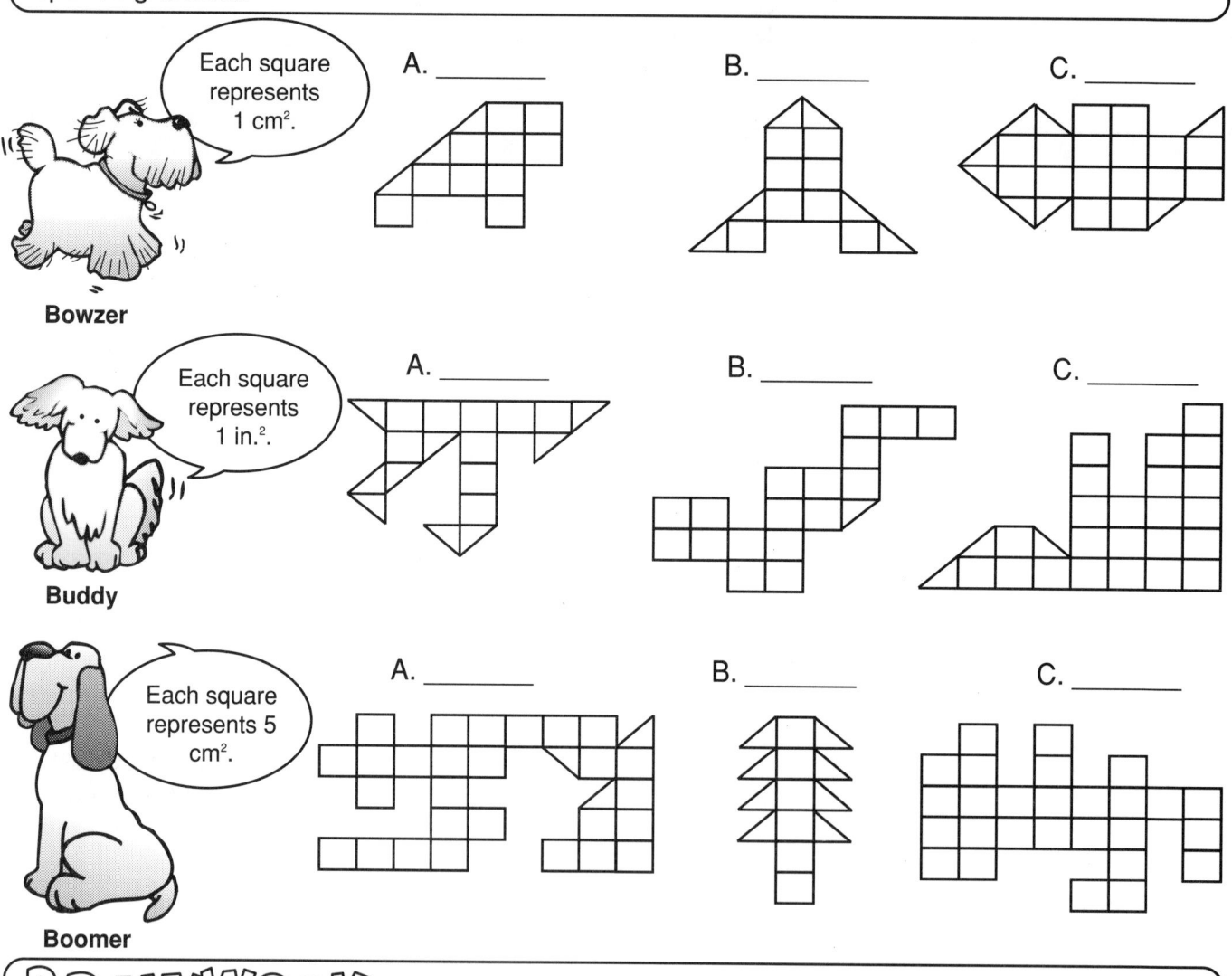

Each square represents 1 cm^2.

A. _____   B. _____   C. _____

Bowzer

Each square represents 1 in.^{2}.

A. _____   B. _____   C. _____

Buddy

Each square represents 5 cm^2.

A. _____   B. _____   C. _____

Boomer

BRAINWORK: A fourth dog, Beamer, also needs more space. Beamer's owner wants his new area to measure about 50 cm^2. Draw a suggested layout on the grid below.

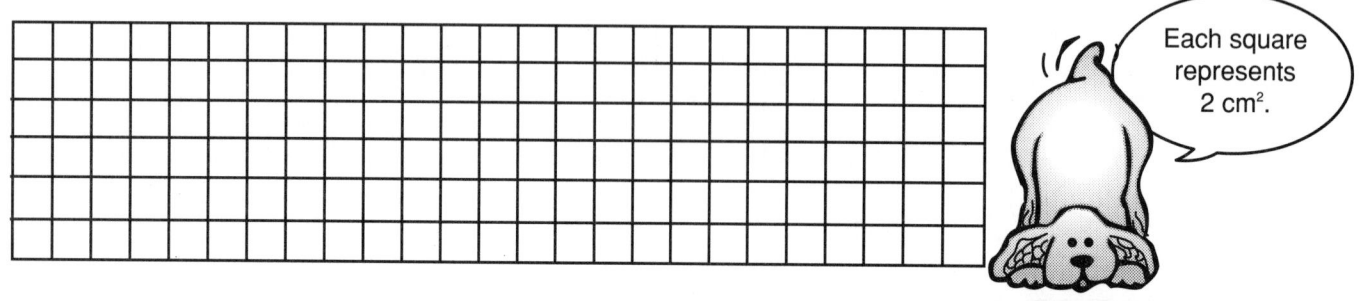

Each square represents 2 cm^2.

Beamer

Name: _____ Power Skill: Finding perimeter

Winning Formations

Coach Crawford is preparing for Saturday's championship soccer game. On each clipboard below, he has drawn 3 different formations for his players. Each formation makes a polygon. The points in each polygon represent where the players will be positioned. Calculate the perimeter of each formation. To find the perimeters of the formations on clipboards 2 and 3, measure the sides of each shape.

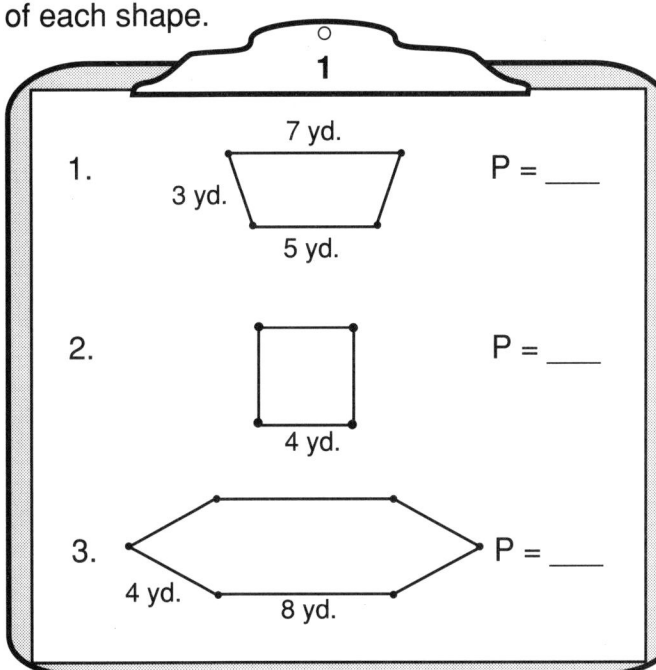

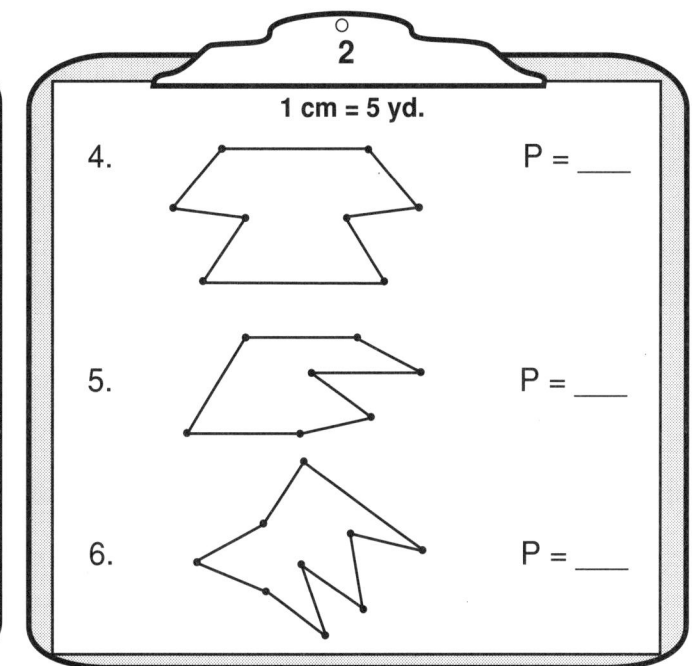

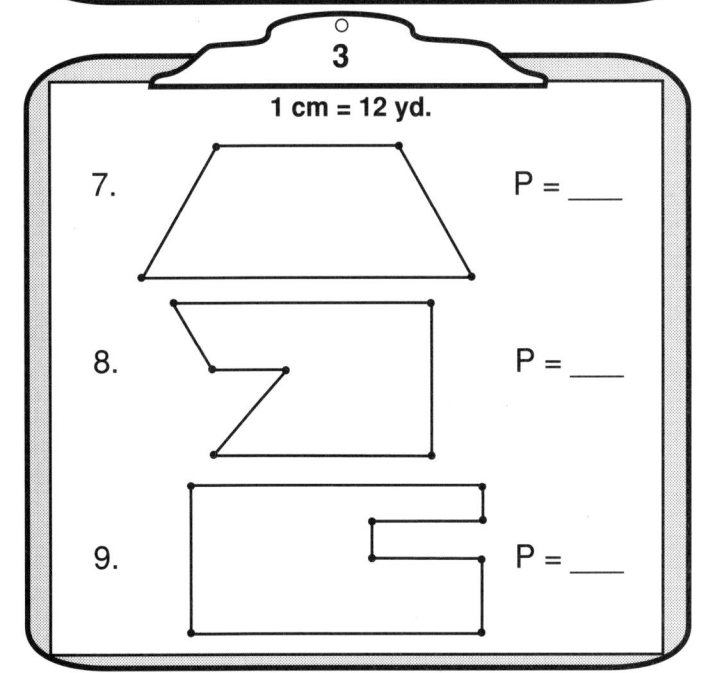

1

1. 7 yd. / 3 yd. / 5 yd.   P = ___

2. 4 yd. (square)   P = ___

3. 4 yd. / 8 yd.   P = ___

2 1 cm = 5 yd.

4. P = ___

5. P = ___

6. P = ___

3 1 cm = 12 yd.

7. P = ___

8. P = ___

9. P = ___

Coach C has decided to include a couple of trick formations. Follow the directions below to determine the perimeter of each one.

A This formation forms a quadrilateral that has an area of 18 yd.² If each side is longer than 1 yard, what are 2 possible perimeters?

B This formation forms a rectangle that has an area of 36 yd.² If each side is longer than 1 yard, what are 4 possible perimeters? On the back of this page, draw and label a shape to represent each perimeter.

BRAINWORK: On the back of this page, draw and label a formation similar to those problems in 4–9 above that Coach C could use with all 11 soccer players. Then trade papers with a friend and measure to help you find the shape's perimeter.

Note to the teacher: Each child will need a metric ruler to complete this page.

Name: _____ Power Skill: Finding area and perimeter

Let the Work Begin!

As Sportsville's new director of buildings and grounds, it's your job to get the new football field ready for play. But there's a lot of work to be done! Fortunately, Hector, your trusty assistant, is willing to help you. Do your calculations on the back of this page. Then write your answers in the blanks provided.

Project Space

Step 1 Calculate the area of the space set aside for the project. _____

Step 2 Order the sod. If it comes in 2 x 3 ft. pieces, how many pieces will be needed?
_____

Step 3 Design the layout. Decide where each item listed below could be positioned in the space at the right. Then draw a shape in the box to represent each item. Make sure you draw each item to scale.

- 40 x 120 yd. football field
- 15 x 30 ft. announcer's booth
- two 20 x 60 yd. bleachers (one on each side of the football field)

1 in. = 40 yd.

Step 4 Now it's time for Hector to chalk the lines on the field. First, he'll outline the field's perimeter. Calculate the perimeter. _____

Step 5 Next, Hector will add 11 yard-line markers. Each marker will be parallel and equal to the field's width. If Hector earns $0.23 per yard, calculate the amount of money he will earn. Then fill in Hector's paycheck below with the total amount of his earnings. Don't forget to include his earnings for marking the field's perimeter!

DATE _____

PAY TO THE ORDER OF _____ $ _____

_____ dollars

Signed _____

BRAINWORK: You think it would be nice to add a 10 x 30 yd. field house for the players. What size rectangle would represent this building on the layout?

©2001 The Education Center, Inc. • Power Practice • Math • TEC2667 • Key p. 108

Note to the teacher: Each child will need a ruler to complete this page.

Name: _____   Power Skill: Finding volume

Packaging Fellogg's Flakes

Franky Fellogg, famous maker of tasty breakfast cereals, is ready to ship his fabulous fruit-flavored flakes to grocery stores all over the country. His shipping company can pack the cereal boxes in the different cartons shown below. Help Franky find the volume of each carton so he'll know which one to use.

Remember: To find volume, multiply length x width x height. Write your answer in cubic units. For example, 3 in. x 4 in. x 2 in. = 24 in.³

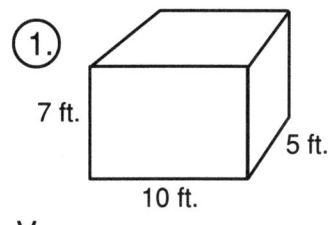

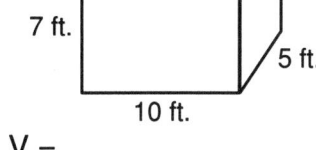

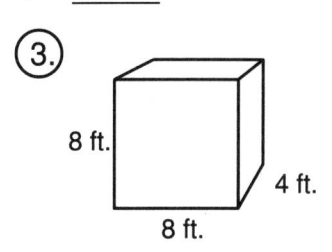

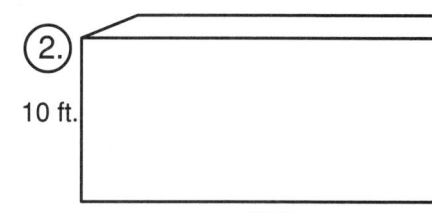

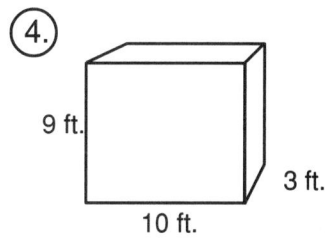

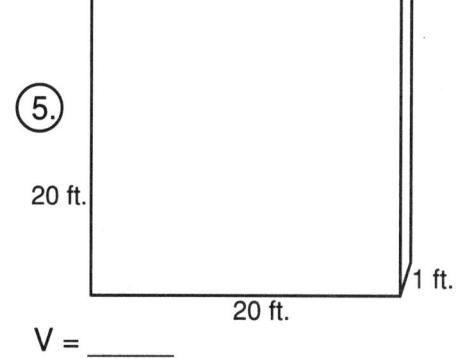

1. 7 ft. x 10 ft. x 5 ft.
V = _____

2. 10 ft. x 25 ft. x 2 ft.
V = _____

3. 8 ft. x 8 ft. x 4 ft.
V = _____

4. 9 ft. x 10 ft. x 3 ft.
V = _____

5. 20 ft. x 20 ft. x 1 ft.
V = _____

6. Which carton has the greatest volume? _____ The least? _____

Franky invented 6 exciting new flavors of his fruit-flavored flakes. He wants to mail free sample boxes of the flakes to millions of families. Circle the box that you think will hold the most cereal. Put a star by the one that you think will hold the least. Then calculate the volume of each box.

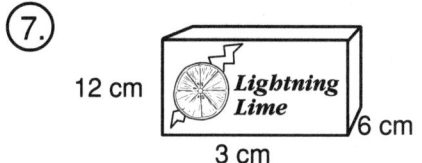

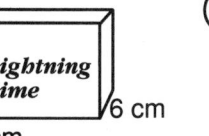

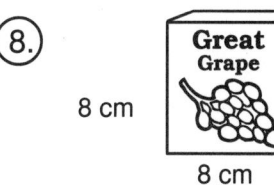

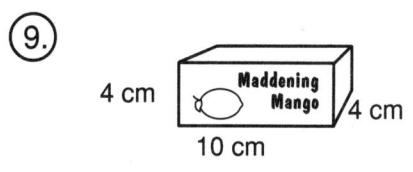

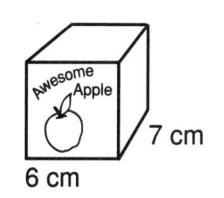

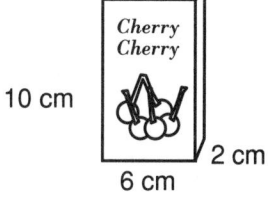

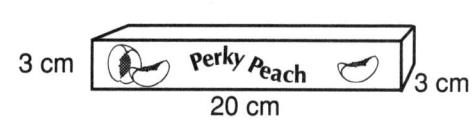

7. Lightning Lime — 12 cm x 3 cm x 6 cm
V = _____

8. Great Grape — 8 cm x 8 cm x 2 cm
V = _____

9. Maddening Mango — 4 cm x 10 cm x 4 cm
V = _____

10. Awesome Apple — 6 cm x 6 cm x 7 cm
V = _____

11. Cherry Cherry — 10 cm x 6 cm x 2 cm
V = _____

12. Perky Peach — 3 cm x 20 cm x 3 cm
V = _____

BRAINWORK: Invent another flavor of Fellogg's Flakes. On the back of this page, draw a box in which the cereal can be shipped. Make the box have different measurements than those used in problems 7–12 above. Then calculate the volume of the box.

©2001 The Education Center, Inc. • Power Practice • Math • TEC2667 • Key p. 109

Name: _____   Power Skill: Finding circumference

Hitting the Mark!

Hit the mark by following the directions below to find the *circumference* (the distance around) of the circles that form the bull's-eye below.

Directions: Cut off the measuring arrow from the right edge of this page. Standing the arrow on its straight edge, bend it along the length of the curved line that forms a circle as shown. When you have measured the length to the nearest centimeter, record it on the corresponding line below. Then find and record the diameter of the circle. Repeat for each circle in the bull's-eye.

How to use the measuring arrow

	Circle	Measured Circumference	Diameter
1.	30 point		
2.	40 point		
3.	50 point		
4.	60 point		
5.	80 point		
6.	bull's-eye		

Calculated Circumference

8. _____
9. _____
10. _____
11. _____
12. _____
13. _____

7. Compare the measurements you recorded above. About how many times larger is each circumference than the diameter? ____ Mathematicians express this relationship in a formula and use it to find the circumference of a circle.

Circumference = π x diameter

Now use the formula C = πd (and 3.14 as π) to calculate the circumference of each circle. Record each corresponding answer in the numbered blanks 8–13 above.

BRAINWORK: On the back of this page, trace 3 different circular objects. Use the measuring arrow to find the diameter of each circle. Then use the formula above to find the circumference of each circle.

©2001 The Education Center, Inc. • *Power Practice* • Math • TEC2667 • Key p. 109

60 **Note to the teacher:** Students will need scissors and a calculator to complete this page.

Name: _____ Power Skill: Finding area of circles

Proving Rodney Right

Mr. Ridley, Rodney's math teacher, often uses riddles to begin his classes. He recently asked the class, "Why do people say pies are squared when they're really round?" Rodney answered, "Because they are—in a math formula for finding the area of circles!" Prove Rodney right by using the formula $A = \pi r^2$ to find the area of the circular objects described below. Round your answers to the nearest hundredth.

To use the formula $A = \pi r^2$, follow these steps:
1. Square the radius (multiply it by itself). If the diameter is the only measurement given, find the radius by dividing the diameter by 2.
2. Multiply the product by π. Use 3.14 for π.
3. Record your answer in square units.

1. cookie with a 1 in. radius _____

2. bicycle wheel with a 2 ft. diameter _____

3. apple pie with a 14 in. diameter _____

4. manhole cover with a 1.75 ft. radius _____

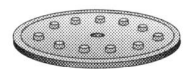

5. CD with a 6 cm radius _____

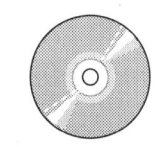

6. coffee mug with an 8 cm diameter _____

7. button with a 1.5 cm diameter _____

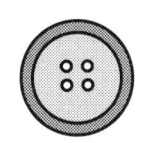

8. clockface with a 4.5 cm radius _____

9. bagel with a 5 in. diameter _____

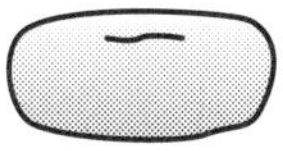

10. skateboard wheel with a 3 cm radius _____

11. can of soup with a 7 cm diameter _____

12. candy dish with a 4.5 cm radius _____

BRAINWORK: Use the formula $C = \pi d$ to find the circumference of each circular object above. Show your work on the back of this page.

©2001 The Education Center, Inc. • Power Practice • Math • TEC2667 • Key p. 109

Note to the teacher: Students will need calculators to complete this page.

Name: _____   Power Skill: Finding probability

Sweet on Probability

Make your mouth water by thinking about pulling candies from a bag! Answer the questions below. Then follow the steps for conducting a probability test to prove your answers.

1. If there are 7 candies in a bag—4 yellow, 2 green, and 1 red—which color of candy are you *least likely* to pull out of the bag in 10 tries? _____ Explain. _____
   _____

2. Which color of candy are you *most likely* to pull out of the bag in 10 tries? _____
   Explain. _____

3. Are you *equally likely* to pull any 2 colors from the bag? Why or why not? _____
   _____

4. What is the probability of pulling a green candy from the bag? _____ A blue candy? _____

Probability Test

1. Color the candy squares at the bottom of the page as follows: 4 of one color, 2 of a second color, and 1 of a third color.

2. Record the 3 colors in the frequency table at the right. Circle the color you think you'd be most likely to pull from a bag in 20 tries. _____

3. Cut out the colored squares and place them in a paper bag.

4. Shake the bag. Without looking inside the bag, pull out 1 paper square.

5. Use a tally mark to record the color of the square in the table's tally column. Then put the square back in the bag.

Color	Tally	Frequency

6. Repeat Steps 4 and 5 20 times. Record the total tallies for each color in the frequency column. Was your prediction in Step 2 correct? _____ Explain your test results. _____
   _____

BRAINWORK: Discard 1 or 2 of your paper squares. On the back of this page, make a frequency table like the one above. Then follow Steps 2, 4, 5, and 6 to repeat the test with your new batch of paper squares.

Name: _____ Power Skill: Using a spinner

Spin 'n' Grin!

Business has been so good at the Spiffy Spinner Company that they're throwing a party for their patrons. Join in the fun by completing the tasks below. You'll have a spinning good time!

Come spin with me!

Task 1: Color each square on the spinner at the left a different color. Use a pencil and a paper clip to make a spinner as shown.

A. What is the probability of spinning each color? _____ How many times do you think you would spin each color in 12 spins? _____

B. Spin the spinner 12 times. Record the outcome of each spin below.

1. _____   4. _____   7. _____   10. _____
2. _____   5. _____   8. _____   11. _____
3. _____   6. _____   9. _____   12. _____

C. Did the outcome in B match your prediction in A? _____ Explain. _____
_____

Task 2: Color any 2 of the squares on the spinner at the right the same color. Use 2 different colors to color the 2 remaining squares.

A. What is the probability of spinning each color? _____ How many times do you think you would spin each color in 12 spins? _____

B. Spin the spinner 12 times. Record the outcome of each spin below.

1. _____   4. _____   7. _____   10. _____
2. _____   5. _____   8. _____   11. _____
3. _____   6. _____   9. _____   12. _____

C. Did the outcome in B match your prediction in A? _____ Explain. _____
_____

BRAINWORK: Make another spinner on the back of this paper. Color 3 squares the same color and the remaining square a different color. Follow Steps A, B, and C from Task 2 above.

Note to the teacher: Each student will need a pencil, a paper clip, and 4 different crayons or markers to complete this page.

Name: _____ **Power Skill:** Using a frequency table

Domino Odds

Cassie and Jake are playing a game with a set of double-6 dominoes. All of the dominoes are facedown on the table. What are the odds that Cassie will draw a tile with exactly 10 pips? Don't fret! Just use Domino Don's tips for solving this problem!

Steps:

1. Use the table below to show all of the possible sums.

2. Think about the tiles in a set of double-6 dominoes. The least possible total of pips is 0 (with the 0-0 tile). The greatest possible total is 12 (with the 6-6 tile). Fill in the table to show the sums for a complete set of dominoes. *(Hint: There are 28 tiles all together.)*

3. Now that the table is complete, go back to the original question: What is the probability that Cassie will draw a tile that has exactly 10 pips? According to the table, there are 2 tiles that have a sum of 10 pips. Her odds are 2 in 28, written $\frac{2}{28}$ (which can be reduced to $\frac{1}{14}$).

4. Write "$\frac{2}{28} = \frac{1}{14}$" in the table's probability column for the sum of 10.

5. Find and record the probability for the remaining sums in the same way.

To solve this problem, just follow the steps!

Sum	Tiles with that sum	Number of tiles	Probability
0	0-0	1	
1	0-1	1	
2	1-1, 2-0	2	
3			
4			
5			
6			
7			
8			
9			
10			
11			
12			

Now use the completed table to find the probability of drawing the following tiles.

1. a domino with a sum of 9 or more _____
2. a domino with a sum less than 5 _____
3. a domino with an even sum _____
4. a double domino, such as 4-4 _____
5. a domino with a sum divisible by 3 _____

BRAINWORK: Follow the same procedure above to determine the number of tiles in a set of double-9 dominoes. Are your chances of drawing the 0-0 tile greater when using a double-6 set or a double-9 set? Why?

Name: _____ Power Skill: Interpreting data

Speaking Up (Statistically) for Sports!

Favorite Sport Day is coming up at school soon. Unfortunately, there is only enough playground space for one sport. Which sport should be played: soccer, baseball, or football? Help your teacher make a decision by completing the tasks below.

1. Survey your classmates to find out which sport each enjoys playing most. Record the results in the frequency table at the right.

2. Display your data in the bar graph below.

Frequency Table

Sport	Tally	Frequency
soccer		
baseball		
football		

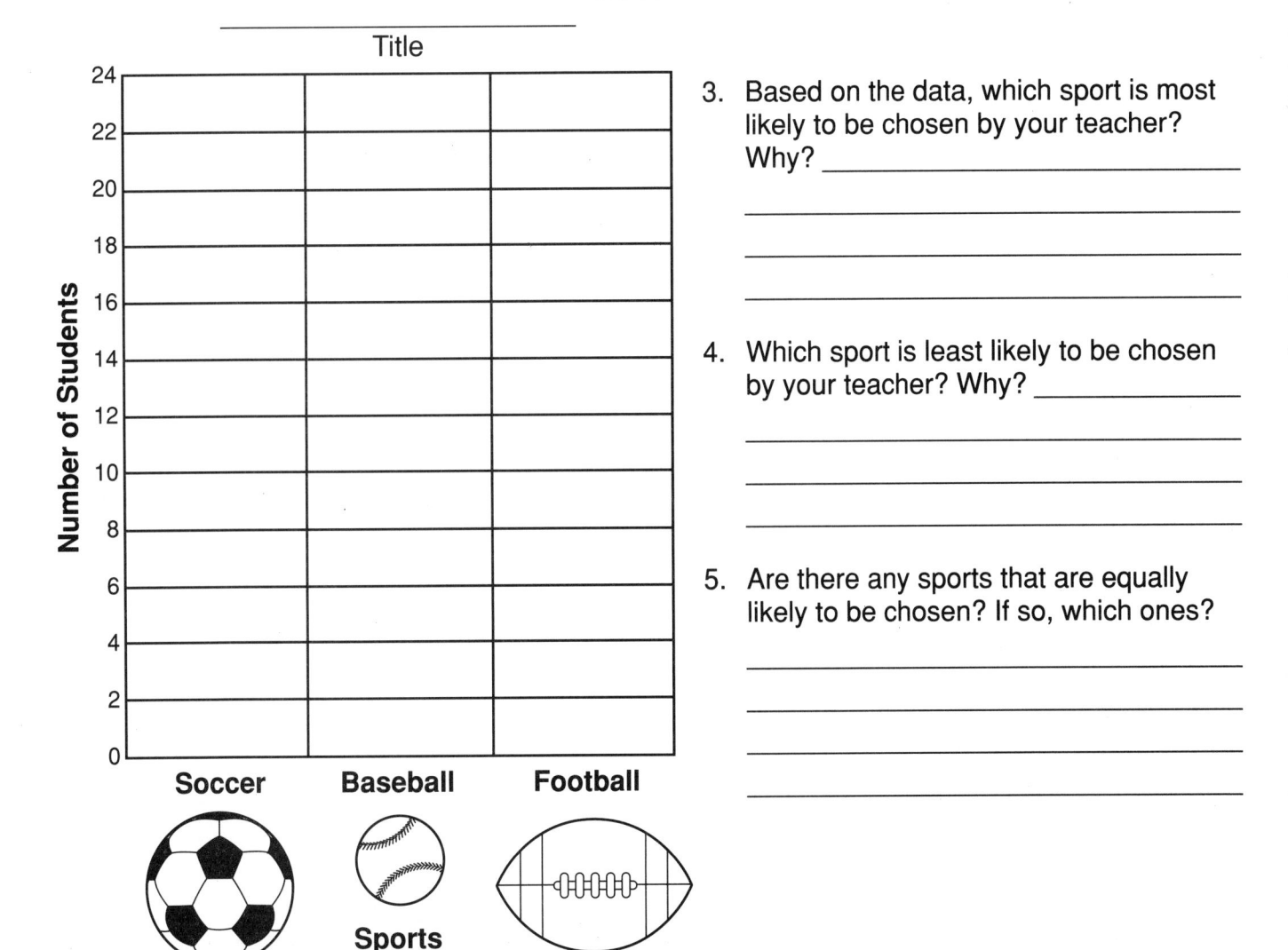

Title: _____

Number of Students (y-axis: 0–24 by 2s)

Sports (x-axis): Soccer, Baseball, Football

3. Based on the data, which sport is most likely to be chosen by your teacher? Why? _____

4. Which sport is least likely to be chosen by your teacher? Why? _____

5. Are there any sports that are equally likely to be chosen? If so, which ones? _____

BRAINWORK: On the back of this page, write 3 sentences explaining why you think collecting data is a fair way to make a decision that could affect many people.

©2001 The Education Center, Inc. • Power Practice • Math • TEC2667

65

Name: _____ Power Skill: Determining the fairness of a game

Was Claire Being Fair?

Claire had a slumber party at her house last weekend. During the party, she had her friends play games to decide which video to watch, what to eat, what to play, and where to sleep. Afterward, her friends said that some of the games weren't fair. Follow the directions below to play the games yourself and decide if her friends were right.

Game 1: Which Video to Watch?

Roll 1 die 1 time.

rolling an even number = comedy
rolling an odd number = mystery

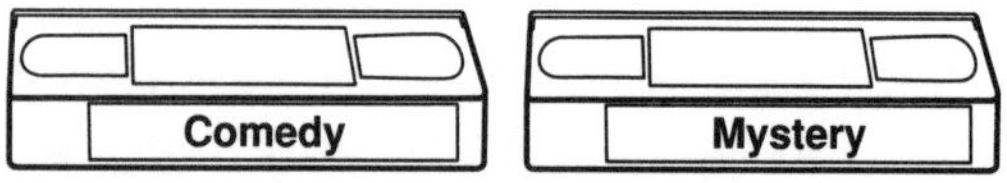

Is this game fair?   YES   NO
Why? _____
_____
_____
_____

Game 2: What to Eat?

Roll a pair of dice 1 time.

rolling a sum 2–9 = pizza
rolling a sum 10–12 = hamburgers

Is this game fair?   YES   NO
Why? (Use an organized list to help you explain your answer.) _____
_____
_____

Game 3: What to Play?

Roll a pair of dice 1 time.

rolling a factor of 12 = cards
rolling any other number = board games

Is this game fair?   YES   NO
Why? (Use an organized list to help you explain your answer.) _____
_____
_____

Game 4: Where to Sleep?

Roll a pair of dice 1 time.

rolling a multiple of 5 = inside
rolling any other number = outside

Is this game fair?   YES   NO
Why? (Use an organized list to help you explain your answer.) _____
_____
_____

BRAINWORK: On the back of this page, create your own dice game for which snack food the girls should have: popcorn or chips. Then have a classmate play the game and decide if your game is fair.

Note to the teacher: Each student will need a pair of dice to complete this page.

Name: _____   Power Skill: Finding mean, median, mode, and range

Not Your Average Meal

Chef Numerales is in the kitchen cooking up his favorite math recipes. Each recipe below includes 7 number ingredients. Find the mean, median, mode, and range of each recipe's set of numbers and record the answers in the blanks below. Round each answer to the nearest tenth.

mean—the sum of a set of numbers divided by how many numbers are in the set
median—the middle number when the set of numbers is listed in order from least to greatest
mode—the number that occurs most often
range—the difference between the greatest number and the least number in a set of numbers

1. Marshmallow Math Salad: 312, 481, 469, 210, 122, 210, 517

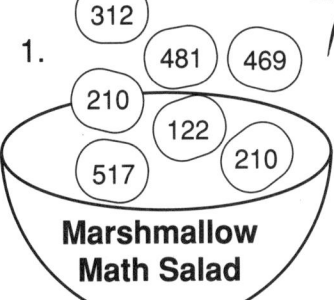

   mean = _____
   median = _____
   mode = _____
   range = _____

2. Spicy Math Meatballs: 150, 200, 10, 250, 50, 300, 50

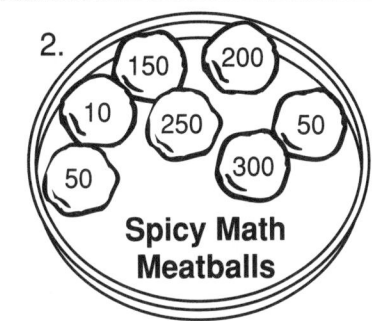

   mean = _____
   median = _____
   mode = _____
   range = _____

3. 123s Stew: 23, 21, 31, 12, 22, 13, 13

   mean = _____
   median = _____
   mode = _____
   range = _____

4. Matharoni Casserole: 2.5, 3, 8.5, 1.5, 3, 5, 4

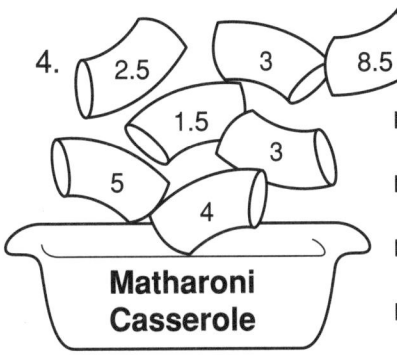

   mean = _____
   median = _____
   mode = _____
   range = _____

5. Mathematized Pizza: 1,060, 818, 818, 2,080, 86, 5, 110

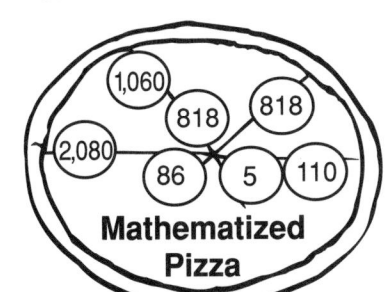

   mean = _____
   median = _____
   mode = _____
   range = _____

6. Math Malted Milk: 48, 45, 49, 49, 49, 49, 46

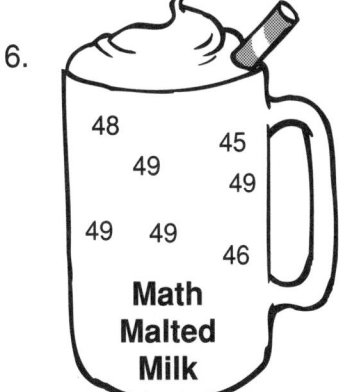

   mean = _____
   median = _____
   mode = _____
   range = _____

BRAINWORK: Create your own math recipe for a Mocha-Math Milk Shake. Include 7 numbers as the ingredients. Then find the mean, median, mode, and range of the numbers.

©2001 The Education Center, Inc. • Power Practice • Math • TEC2667 • Key p. 109

Note to the teacher: Each student will need a calculator to complete this page.

67

Name: ______________________ **Power Skill:** Reading and interpreting a bar graph

Hockey Champion Hopefuls

The youth hockey season in Anytown, USA, is winding down. The coaches have posted the total goals scored by each team in the form of a graph. They hope the public will use the data to predict the winner of the upcoming hockey championship games. Use the graph to answer the questions below.

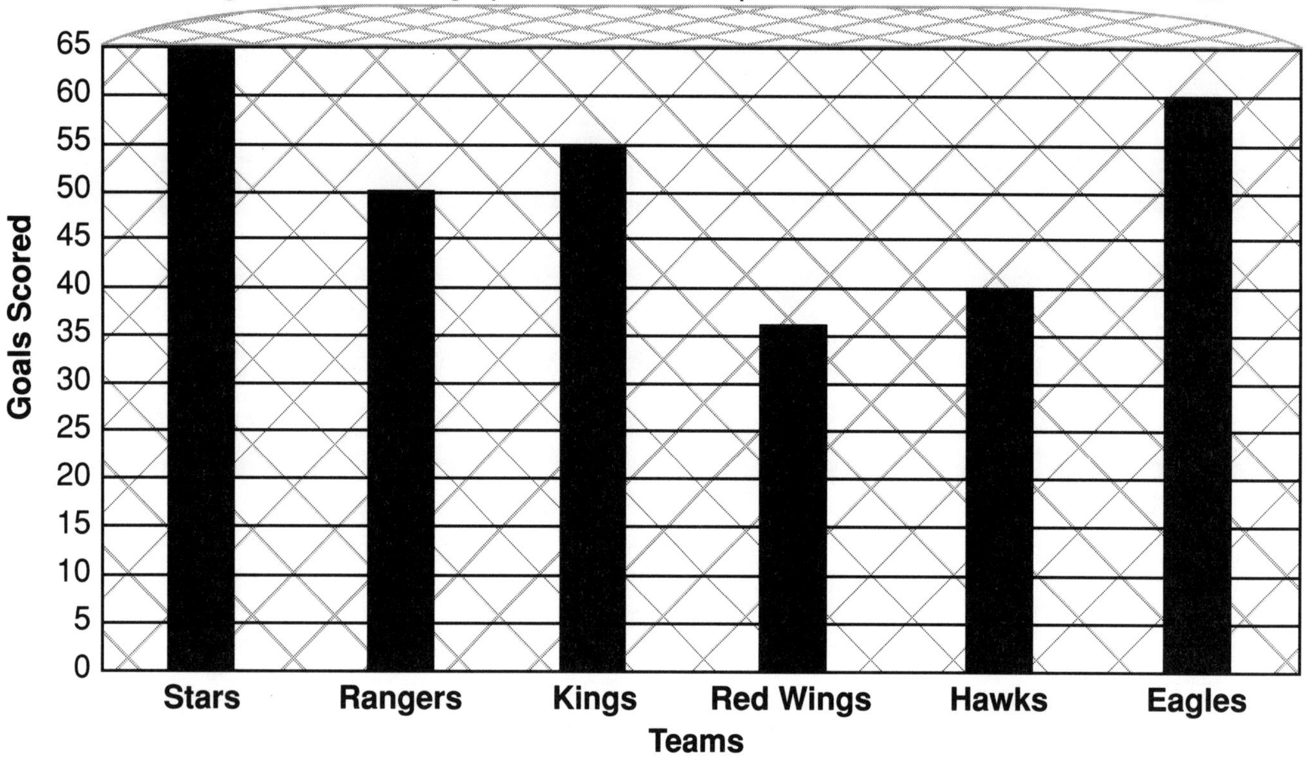

1. How many goals did each team score during the regular season?
   Stars _____ Kings _____ Hawks _____
   Rangers _____ Red Wings _____ Eagles _____
2. List the teams and their number of goals in order from least to greatest. ________________
   ____
3. What is the total number of goals scored by the teams? __________
4. What is the average number of goals scored during the regular season? __________
5. If the Stars played 12 games during their regular season, what was the average number of goals they scored in each game? __________
6. What is the difference between the number of highest and lowest goals scored? __________
7. How many more goals did the Eagles score than the Red Wings? __________
8. How many more goals would the Hawks had to have scored in order to be tied with the Kings? To have more goals than the Kings but fewer than the Stars? __________

BRAINWORK: Based on the data in the graph, which 2 teams do you think will play each other in the finals? Write your prediction on the back of this page. Give 3 reasons to support your answer.

©2001 The Education Center, Inc. • *Power Practice • Math* • TEC2667 • Key p. 109

Name: _____ Power Skill: Constructing a bar graph

Afterschool Fun

What do your classmates most like to do for fun after school? Conduct a survey to find out!

Directions: Use a tally mark to record each student's response in the boxes below. Then use the data to complete the bar graph at the bottom of the page.

Play sports	Ride bike/scooter	Skate/Skateboard	Read/write
Play/listen to music	Draw/paint	Talk with friends	Use computer/watch TV

Afterschool Fun

Activities

	2	4	6	8	10	12	14	16	18	20	22	24	26	28	30
Play sports															
Ride bike/scooter															
Skate/skateboard															
Read/write															
Play/listen to music															
Draw/paint															
Talk with friends															
Use computer/watch TV															

Students

BRAINWORK: On the back of this page or on another sheet of paper, write 5 questions that could be answered using your graph.

©2001 The Education Center, Inc. • Power Practice • Math • TEC2667

Name: _____ **Power Skill:** Reading, interpreting pictographs

Recyclathons Rule!

Greene County just had a fantastic recyclathon! Three towns in the county were involved, recycling as much garbage as they could. After 1 month, all the recycled materials were weighed. The town with the most recyclables in pounds won an award.

Directions: Use the pictograph to answer the questions below about the recyclathon.

Greene County Recyclathon

Greenville   Garbageton   Mt. Trashmore

(can)	10 pounds of aluminum
(newspaper)	100 pounds of paper
(jug)	10 pounds of plastic
(jar)	10 pounds of glass
(box)	10 pounds of cardboard

1. How many pounds of aluminum did each town collect?
   a. Greenville _____   b. Garbageton _____   c. Mt. Trashmore _____

2. How many pounds of paper did each town collect?
   a. Greenville _____   b. Garbageton _____   c. Mt. Trashmore _____

3. Who collected the most glass? _____
   The least? _____

4. How much more cardboard did Greenville collect than Garbageton? _____

5. How much plastic was collected by all 3 towns?
   _____

6. Which product do you think Mt. Trashmore might really like?
   a. toothpaste   b. soda pop   c. magazines

Fill out the award certificate for the winning town.

1st Congratulations to _____, the town that collected the most recyclables: _____ pounds!

BRAINWORK: Only $\frac{2}{3}$ of the citizens of Mt. Trashmore participated in the recyclathon. How many total pounds of recycled materials could Mt. Trashmore have recycled if everyone had been involved?

Name: _____ Power Skill: Constructing pictographs

Mr. Moore's Reading List

Mr. Reid Moore is encouraging his class—25 students in all—to read some good books. He's already made a list of books. Mr. Moore knows how many of his students have read each book on his list, and he would like to post the information.

Directions: Using the information below, construct a pictograph showing how many of Mr. Moore's students have read each book.

Books	Number of Readers
The Phantom Tollbooth	
The Wind in the Willows	
Where the Red Fern Grows	
The Secret Garden	
Little Women	

Key: 📖 = 2 students

Reading List

The Phantom Tollbooth has been read by 15 students.

The Wind in the Willows has been read by 9 students.

Where the Red Fern Grows has been read by 13 students.

The Secret Garden has been read by 6 students.

Little Women has been read by 12 students.

BRAINWORK: Use a calculator to determine the percentage of Mr. Moore's students who have read each book.

Name: _____ Power Skill: Reading, interpreting line graphs

Sweet Stuff Candy Company

Congratulations! You are the new sales manager for Sweet Stuff Candy Company. Examine the company's sales figures on the line graph below in order to make an informed report to the company's president, Ms. Candy Sellers.

Sweet Stuff Candy Company Sales
(In thousands of dollars)

1. What were the 4 highest sales months? List the months and the amounts sold, with the highest month listed first.
   _____
   _____
   _____
   _____

2. What were the 4 lowest months? List the months and the amounts sold, with the lowest month listed first.
   _____
   _____
   _____
   _____

3. In what month(s) did the company sell exactly $35,000 worth of candy? _____

4. Look at the highs and lows on the graph. How would you explain to Ms. Sellers why some months are so high and others are so low? _____

5. Would you recommend spending more money on advertising during June or November? Explain your answer. _____

6. What was the total amount of sales for the year? _____

BRAINWORK: In thousands of dollars, what was the mean monthly sales for the graphed year?

Name: _____   Power Skill: Constructing line graphs

Keeping Tabs on Television

Frances and Fiona were in hog heaven when their parents allowed them to have televisions in their rooms. However, their parents told them they had to keep track of any time they spent watching television.

Directions: Create a line graph to track the time that Frances and Fiona watch television. Use a blue colored pencil to track Frances's time and a red one to track Fiona's time.

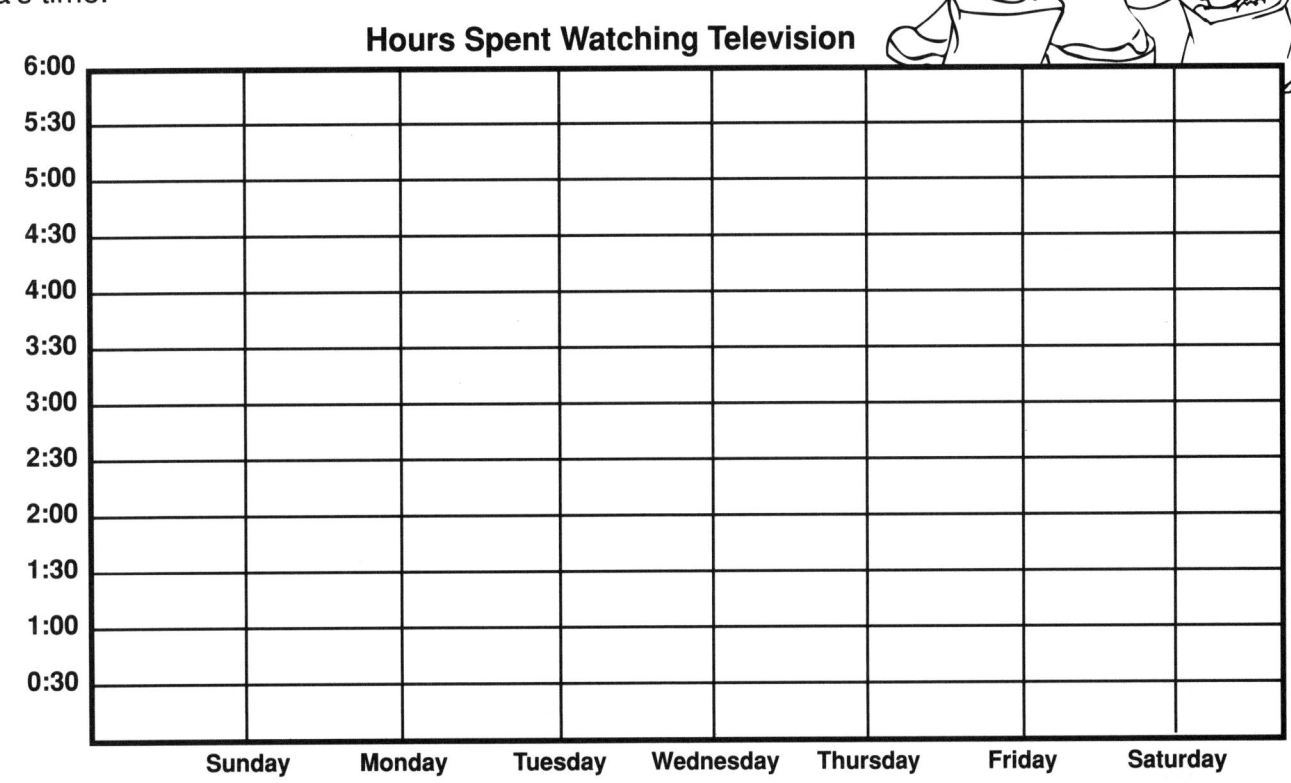

Hours Spent Watching Television

(Y-axis: 0:30 to 6:00 in 30-minute increments; X-axis: Sunday, Monday, Tuesday, Wednesday, Thursday, Friday, Saturday)

	Frances's TV Time	Fiona's TV Time
Sunday	3:30	2:00
Monday	2:00	1:00
Tuesday	3:00	1:30
Wednesday	1:00	2:00
Thursday	4:30	3:00
Friday	0:30	2:30
Saturday	3:30	1:00

BRAINWORK: On the back of this paper, construct a line graph to illustrate how much time you spend reading each day for 1 week.

©2001 The Education Center, Inc. • Power Practice • Math • TEC2667 • Key p. 110

Note to the teacher: Each child will need a copy of this page, 1 blue colored pencil, and 1 red colored pencil.

73

Name: _____   Power Skill: Reading, interpreting circle graphs

All Scream for Ice Cream

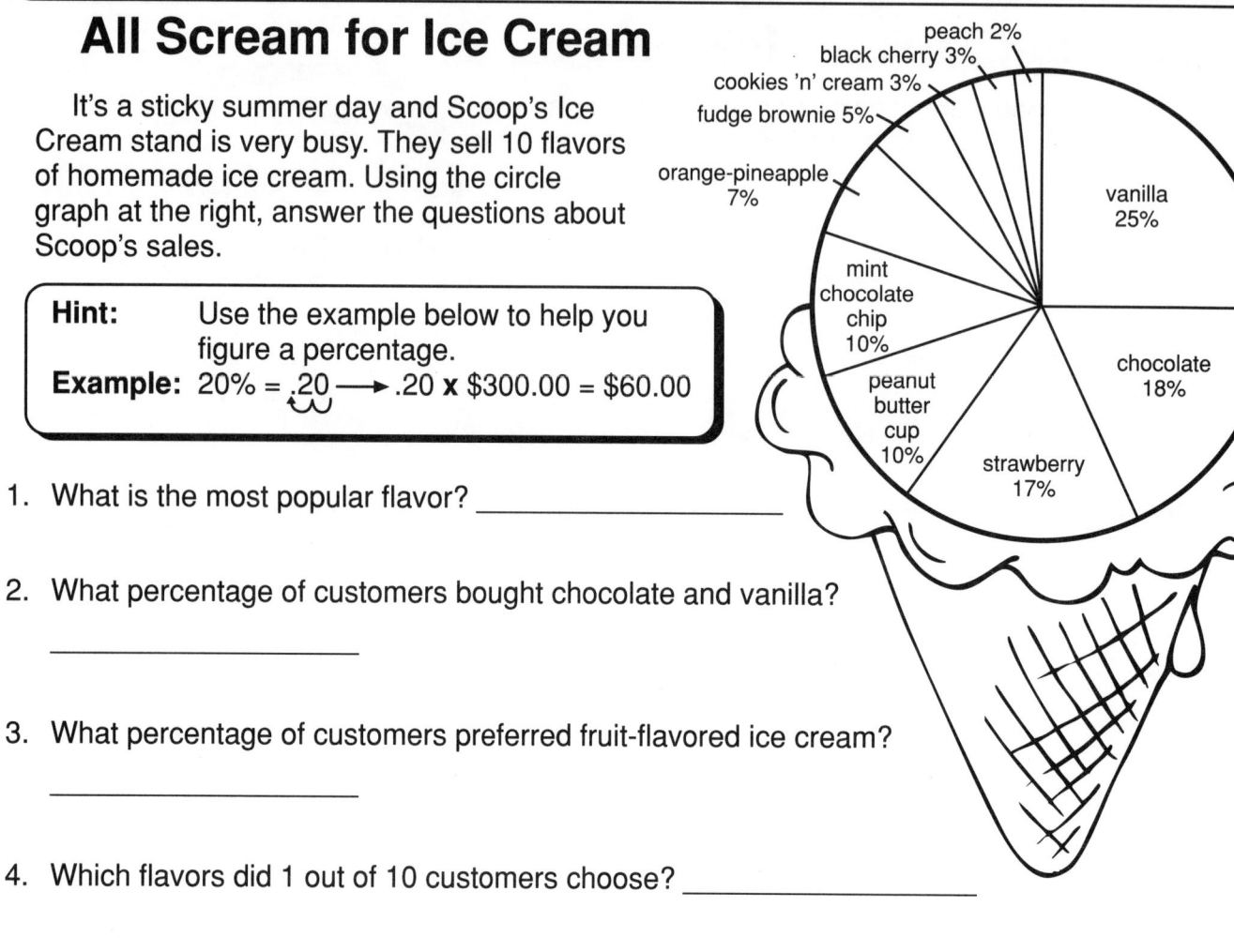

It's a sticky summer day and Scoop's Ice Cream stand is very busy. They sell 10 flavors of homemade ice cream. Using the circle graph at the right, answer the questions about Scoop's sales.

Hint: Use the example below to help you figure a percentage.
Example: 20% = .20 → .20 x $300.00 = $60.00

Circle graph flavors:
- peach 2%
- black cherry 3%
- cookies 'n' cream 3%
- fudge brownie 5%
- orange-pineapple 7%
- mint chocolate chip 10%
- peanut butter cup 10%
- strawberry 17%
- chocolate 18%
- vanilla 25%

1. What is the most popular flavor? _____

2. What percentage of customers bought chocolate and vanilla?
   _____

3. What percentage of customers preferred fruit-flavored ice cream?
   _____

4. Which flavors did 1 out of 10 customers choose? _____

5. If Scoop's had 100 customers on August 6, how many customers ordered mint chocolate chip? _____ Orange-pineapple and peach? _____ Vanilla? _____

6. If Scoop's made $300.00 on August 6, how much money was made from sales of peanut butter cup? _____ Fudge brownie? _____ The top 3 flavors? _____

7. How much profit would Scoop's make if all his ingredients cost him $35.00? _____

8. If you were at Scoop's, what flavor would you choose? _____

9. What percentage of Scoop's customers have the same taste as you? _____

BRAINWORK: Scoop's made $200.00 on September 6. Make a circle graph that shows how much money was made on each flavor.

74   ©2001 The Education Center, Inc. • Power Practice • Math • TEC2667 • Key p. 110

Name: _____   Power Skill: Constructing circle graphs

Laugh Graphs!

Rita, the roving raccoon reporter, has been telling jokes to a pack of laughing hyenas and then surveying their favorite kinds. Read the information in each box and then complete a circle laugh graph for each survey. Remember that each graph should include a title and labels.

Q: When should a baker stop making doughnuts?
A: When he gets tired of the *hole* business!

1. Rita found that in a group of adult female hyenas, $\frac{1}{2}$ of the group preferred knock-knock jokes, $\frac{1}{4}$ preferred elephant jokes, $\frac{1}{8}$ preferred puns, and $\frac{1}{8}$ preferred waiter jokes.

"Why did the elephant paint his toenails different colors?"
"I don't know. Why?"
"So he could hide in the M&M's®!"

2. Rita also surveyed a group of 100 adult male hyenas. Fifty male hyenas said that waiter jokes were their favorite, 20 preferred knock-knock jokes, 10 preferred elephant jokes, and 20 preferred puns.

"Waiter, waiter, what's that fly doing in my soup?"
"Looks like the backstroke, sir."

3. Finally, Rita surveyed a group of young hyenas, both male and female. She found that $\frac{3}{10}$ of them liked elephant jokes the most, while the knock-knock jokes, waiter jokes, and puns each received $\frac{1}{5}$ of the votes. A final $\frac{1}{10}$ of the young hyenas simply didn't understand any of the jokes.

BRAINWORK: Ask at least 10 people to name their favorite kinds of jokes. Use the categories already mentioned. On the back of this page, chart your results. Then make a circle graph. Remember to label and title it.

Name: _____   Power Skill: Reading and interpreting stem-and-leaf plots

Presidential Plotting

A stem-and-leaf plot shows data organized by place value. The tens digit is called the stem. The ones digits are called leaves.

Example: 2 | 2 4 5 represents 22, 24, and 25.

Directions: Answer the following questions using the presidential stem-and-leaf plot.

Ages of presidents when they were inaugurated, since 1900:

Stem	Leaves
4	2 3 6
5	1 1 1 2 4 4 5 5 6 6
6	0 1 2 4 9

1. What is the youngest age for a president to be inaugurated since 1900? _____

2. When inaugurated, how many presidents since 1900 have been in their 50s? _____

3. What is the difference in ages from the oldest to the youngest (range)? _____

4. How many presidents have been inaugurated since 1900? _____

5. Which age appears the most often (mode) in this stem-and-leaf plot? _____

6. How many of the presidents that have been inaugurated since 1900 have been younger than 40? _____

7. Which age is the mean (average)? _____

BRAINWORK: Use the data in the stem-and-leaf plot to create a bar graph. Don't forget labels and a title.

Name: _____   Power Skill: Constructing stem-and-leaf plots

Sizing Up Stem-and-Leaf Plots

The Petersville Little League players need uniforms. The team manager is measuring the height of the players to make sure they get the right sizes. Help the team manager organize the players' heights by constructing a stem-and-leaf plot.

Part I: Use the data to construct a stem-and-leaf plot.

Heights of Players (in inches)

49	52	61	52
63	55	60	58
61	62	56	57
54	61	57	59
55	48	58	

Title: _____

Stems	Leaves

Part II: Use the stem-and-leaf plot above and the chart below to answer the following questions.

Uniform Size

Height (inches)	S	M	L	XL
	48–52	53–56	57–60	61–64

1. What is the median height (the middle number in a set of numbers ordered from least to greatest)? _____ inches

2. What height occurred most often (mode)? _____ inches

3. All of the players measured between _____ and _____ inches.

4. The range (the difference between the least and the greatest numbers) of heights is _____.

5. How many players will need small uniforms? _____ Extra large? _____

6. Which size uniform will be needed most? _____

BRAINWORK: Convert the heights of the shortest player and the tallest player into feet and inches.

Name: _____ **Power Skill:** Choosing the appropriate graph

Graphing Spot

Seymour loves to keep track of his new puppy, Spot. He organizes all of Spot's information into tables. Seymour wants to show Spot's data in graphs, but he can't decide which kind of graph to use for each set of data.

Directions: Study each table below. Then decide which kind of graph would best display its data. Complete each graph in the space provided, including labels and titles.

Weight

months	weight
1	12 lb.
2	15 lb.
3	20 lb.
4	25 lb.
5	33 lb.
6	40 lb.

Money

A total of $300.00 was spent.

Food $50.00
Medical $50.00
Toys $25.00
Replacing Shoes $75.00
Bedding/Supplies ... $100.00

Walks

weeks	times walked
1	5
2	6
3	2
4	4
5	1
6	5

Behavior

In one month
Spot scratched .... 85 times
Spot lay on the furniture .... 100 times
Spot chewed on a shoe .... 10 times
Spot chased his tail .... 55 times

Bar graph title: _____

Line graph title: _____

Pictograph title: _____

Circle graph title: _____

BRAINWORK: Many times the same information can be shown on more than 1 kind of graph. Which of Spot's data could be shown on another kind of graph? Why?

78   ©2001 The Education Center, Inc. • Power Practice • Math • TEC2667 • Key p. 110

Name: _____

Power Skill: Working backward

Backtracking

The Racing Rabbits are the fastest track team around! Use the working-backward strategy to solve each problem below.

1. Rita arrived at the track at 2:35 P.M. She missed 5 minutes of practice. Practice began 20 minutes later than scheduled. What time was practice scheduled to begin? _____

2. During a week of practice, Rufus ran the most miles on the team. Roberta ran $\frac{1}{3}$ as many miles as Rufus. Ray ran 6 miles less than Roberta. Rhonda ran 3 miles more than Ray. If Rhonda ran 8 miles, how many miles did Rufus run? _____

3. On the day of the track meet, a news reporter interviewed the coach and recorded each runner's age. Rufus is 3 years older than Ray. Ray is the same age as Rhonda. Rhonda is 2 years older than Rex. Rex is $\frac{3}{4}$ as old as Roberta. Roberta is 1 year younger than Rita. If Rita is 13 years old, how old is each team member? _____

4. Rex had a busy day! He competed in the hurdle race 45 minutes before the meet ended. An hour before that, he watched Roberta compete in the 50-yard dash. Twenty minutes before Roberta's race, Rex ran the relay. Rex arrived at the track meet 35 minutes before the relay race. If the track meet ended at 4:15 P.M., what time did Rex arrive? _____

5. The coach planned a victory party for the team. He bought invitations for $4.95 and then spent 3 times that amount on refreshments. He also spent $45.75 on trophies. If the coach had $4.50 left, how much money did he start with? _____

BRAINWORK! Imagine that a new runner has joined the team. Use the information in problem 3 to write a clue about the runner's age. Give it to a classmate to solve.

©2001 The Education Center, Inc. • Power Practice • Math • TEC2667 • Key p. 110

79

Name: _____   Power Skill: Working backward

Hefty Veggies

It's Hefty Veggie Day at the county fair. People from far and wide have come to enter their huge vegetables in the contest. Contestants with the heaviest vegetables win first prize. The vegetables have been weighed. It's time for you to determine the winners!

Directions: Read each clue. In the space provided, write the name of the winner and the weight of the winning vegetable. Be sure to label each weight in pounds or ounces.

1. Zach's zucchini weighed twice as much as Zazzu's. Zazzu's zucchini weighed 3 times as much as Zoe's. Zoe's zucchini weighed $\frac{1}{2}$ as much as Zelda's. Zelda's zucchini weighed 4 pounds.
   First place: _____   Weight: _____

2. Peggy's pumpkin was 4 pounds heavier than Paul's. Paul's pumpkin was $\frac{1}{5}$ as heavy as Patty's. Patty's pumpkin was $\frac{1}{2}$ as heavy as Pablo's. Pablo's pumpkin was twice as heavy as Peter's. Peter's pumpkin weighed 10 pounds.
   First place: _____   Weight: _____

3. Betsy's beet weighed $\frac{1}{2}$ as much as Byron's. Byron's beet was 4 ounces lighter than Bertha's. Bertha's beet was twice as heavy as Bethany's. Bethany's beet was twice as heavy as Bonnie's. Bonnie's beet weighed 6 ounces.
   First place: _____   Weight: _____

4. Opie's onion was 5 times as heavy as Orville's. Orville's onion was $\frac{1}{3}$ as heavy as Oscar's. Oscar's onion was 9 times heavier than Olivia's. Olivia's onion was twice as heavy as Otis's. Otis's onion weighed 1 ounce.
   First place: _____   Weight: _____

5. Flora's eggplant weighed 1 pound less than Cora's. Cora's eggplant weighed $\frac{1}{2}$ as much as Mora's. Mora's eggplant weighed 8 pounds more than Dora's. Dora's eggplant weighed $\frac{1}{2}$ as much as Nora's. Nora's eggplant weighed 4 pounds.
   First place: _____   Weight: _____

BRAINWORK: Choose 1 of the problems above. On the back of this sheet, draw each contestant in the problem with his or her vegetable. Label each vegetable with its correct weight.

Name: _____   Power Skill: Using logic

Scheduling Solutions

Mrs. Twizzle printed each of her students' schedules on her computer. Unfortunately, the ✔s and Xs that mark the time period for each class did not print out. Use the clues below to complete each student's schedule. Put a ✔ in each box that is true and an X in each box that is not true.

Student A

Clue 1: Science is 2 periods after math.
Clue 2: Social studies immediately follows technology.
Clue 3: English is 4th period.

	1st period	2nd period	3rd period	4th period	5th period
Science					
Math					
English					
Technology					
Social studies					

	1st period	2nd period	3rd period	4th period	5th period
Science					
Math					
English					
Technology					
Social studies					

Student B

Clue 1: Student B was late for his 1st period class, 2nd period social studies class, and science class.
Clue 2: English is sometime after science and sometime before technology.

Student C

Clue 1: Student C has only 2 subjects after technology.
Clue 2: Student C's favorite subjects are social studies, English, and the subject she has last.
Clue 3: Science is immediately before technology.
Clue 4: Student C forgot her books for English and her 4th period class.

	1st period	2nd period	3rd period	4th period	5th period
Science					
Math					
English					
Technology					
Social studies					

BRAINWORK: Use the information above with the following clues to identify Student A, Student B, and Student C: Rob and Rick have social studies at the same time. Renee and Rick have English or math during first period.

Name: _____   Power Skill: Using logic

Reasoning Roundup

Mary Lou, Billy, Chuck, and Dottie are all members of the Reasoning Riding Club. Each member has a riding lesson on a different day of the week. Each member also grooms his or her horse daily at a different time. Use Clues 1–4 to sort out each friend's schedule. Then use Clues 5–7 to determine the name of each member's horse. Put a ✔ in each box that is true and an X in each box that is not true.

Clue 1: The boys have riding lessons on Monday and Tuesday.
Clue 2: Chuck grooms his horse later in the day than Mary Lou.
Clue 3: Dottie and the boy who has riding lessons on Monday groom their horses later in the day than Chuck.
Clue 4: The girl who has riding lessons on Thursday grooms her horse at 1:00 P.M.
Clue 5: One member's first name begins with the same first letters as his horse's name.
Clue 6: Lady's brothers are Rex and the horse that is groomed last.
Clue 7: Lady and the horse that is ridden on Monday are less than 4 years old.

	Riding Lesson Day				Grooming Time				Horse			
	Monday	Tuesday	Wednesday	Thursday	9:00	10:00	11:00	1:00	Rex	Charlie	Lady	Gus
Mary Lou												
Billy												
Chuck												
Dottie												

BRAINWORK: Create a new logic problem to match each horse with its hair color. Give the problem to a classmate to solve.

Name: _____   Power Skill: Using guess and check

Racing for a Solution

Welcome to Solution Speedway! Read each set of clues. Use the guess-and-check strategy to find each race car's number. Then write the number in the space provided.

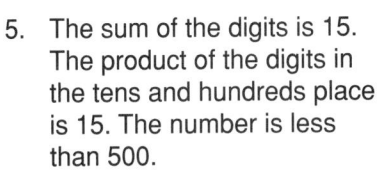

1. The product of the digits is 24. The number is odd.

2. The number is divisible by 5. The sum of the digits is 12.

3. The product of the digits is 36. The number is divisible by 7.

4. The sum of the digits is 12. The product of the digits in the tens and ones place is 16. The number is divisible by 2.

5. The sum of the digits is 15. The product of the digits in the tens and hundreds place is 15. The number is less than 500.

6. The product of the digits is 24. The number is a palindrome.

7. The product of the digits is 8. The number is a palindrome. It is even.

8. The product of the digits is 27. The sum of the digits is 9.

9. The sum of the digits is 11. All of the digits are prime. The number is divisible by 5. Two of the digits are the same.

10. The product of the digits is 0. The sum of the digits is 8. The number is not divisible by 10. The number is greater than 660.

BRAINWORK:
Write 5 consecutive one-digit numbers in the following arrangement so that the sum of each row equals 15.

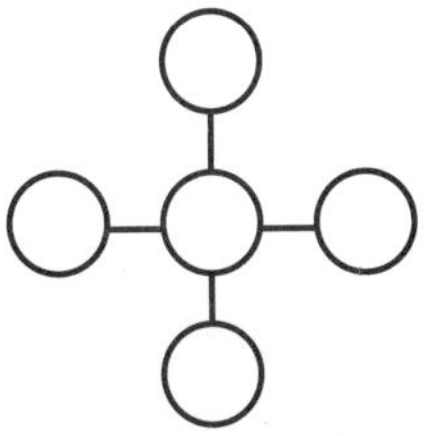

©2001 The Education Center, Inc. • Power Practice • Math • TEC2667 • Key p. 111

Note to the teacher: Remind students that a *palindrome* reads the same forward and backward. Some examples include 3,113 and 434.

Name: _____   Power Skill: Using guess and check

Mixed-Up Muffin Man

Marvin the Muffin Man is in a marvelous mess! Five customers are waiting for their muffins, but Marvin has their orders all mixed up! Marvin knows that his customers ordered the same number of large and small muffins all together. He also knows how much money each person paid. Use the guess-and-check strategy to help Marvin figure out how many muffins each person ordered. Write the answers in the chart below.

Muffin Menu
Large Muffins $0.50
Small Muffins $0.20

Customer	Amount Paid	Number of Large Muffins Bought	Number of Small Muffins Bought
Angry Alice	$2.10		
Frustrated Frank	$1.00		
Sour Sam	$2.00		
Irritable Irene	$0.20		
Raging Roger	$2.40		

How many large muffins did Marvin's customers buy all together? _____

How many small muffins did they buy? _____

BRAINWORK: Describe how to check your work for this problem.

Name: _____   **Power Skill:** Making an organized list

Travel Choices

Tommy Tourist is on his way to a sunny vacation getaway! For each problem below, make an organized list of his travel choices. (Hint: You may use abbreviations when writing your list.)

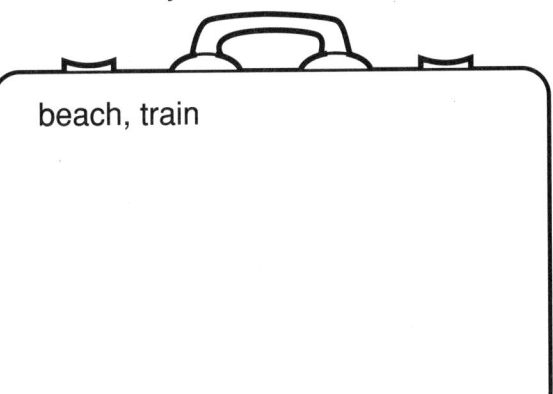

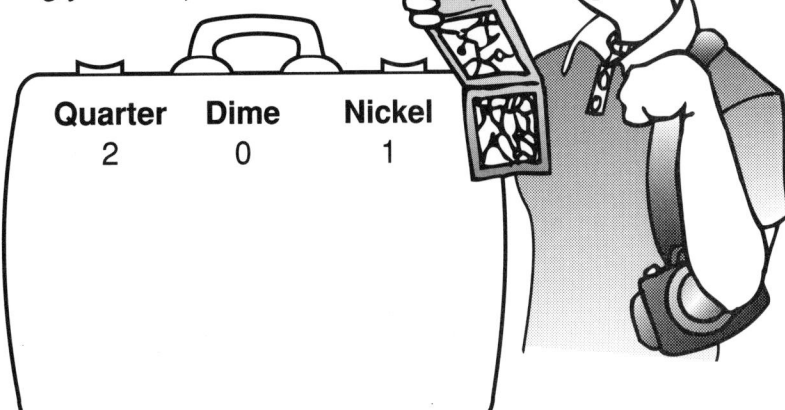

beach, train

Quarter	Dime	Nickel
2	0	1

1. Tommy can go to the beach, the mountains, or a theme park. He can travel by train, plane, or car. List all the combinations of locations and types of transportation. The list has been started for you.

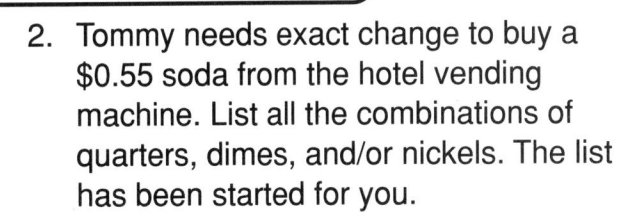

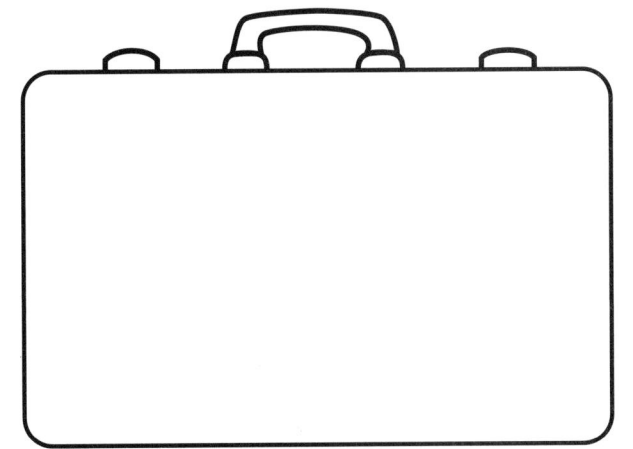

2. Tommy needs exact change to buy a $0.55 soda from the hotel vending machine. List all the combinations of quarters, dimes, and/or nickels. The list has been started for you.

3. Tommy decided to go out for pizza. The menu offers thick or thin crust. His topping choices include pepperoni, sausage, mushroom, or no topping. He can order regular cheese or extra cheese. List all the combinations of crust, topping, and cheese.

4. At the end of his vacation, Tommy started to miss his brother and sister. He decided to contact each of them and then buy each a souvenir. He can contact them by phone, postcard, or email. He can buy a T-shirt, baseball cap, or key chain. List all the combinations of contact and souvenir choices for each sibling.

BRAINWORK: Reread problem 3. Describe the probability of choosing a pizza with a topping as likely, unlikely, or equally likely. Write a fraction to represent the probability.

Name: _____   Power Skill: Making an organized list

Merlin's Magic Shop

Take the mystery out of problem solving with the make-a-list strategy! Help Merlin organize the items in his magic shop by making an organized list for each problem. Then use the price list to answer each question. Complete your lists on the back of this page.

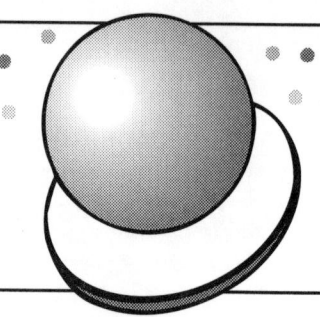

Price List

Magic Carpets
Basic carpet—$15.00
Add $2.00 for high-flying carpets.
Add $3.00 for fast carpets.
Take $1.00 off plaid carpets.

Clothes
Items printed with stars—$8.00
Items printed with lightning bolts—$8.50
Items printed with crystal balls—$7.00

Magician's Starter Kits
Each kit—$20.00
Add $5.00 to kits with gold wands.
Take $10.00 off kits with purple capes.

1. Merlin sells wizard hats and robes printed with stars, lightning bolts, or crystal balls. Make a list of all of the hat and robe outfits that he sells.

   How many outfits cost $16.00 or more? _____

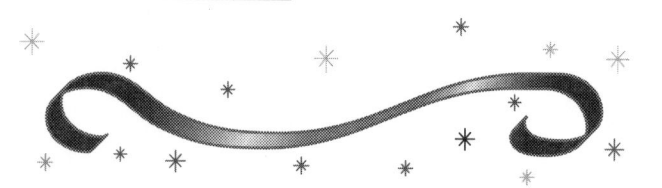

2. Merlin sells a variety of magic carpets. He sells them in red, black, and plaid. His customers may choose fast, slow, or medium carpets. They may choose high-flying or low-flying carpets. List all the types of carpets Merlin sells.

   How many carpets cost $15.00? ____
   More than $15.00? ____
   Less than $15.00? ____

3. Merlin sells a magician's starter kit that includes 1 type of magic potion, a wand, and a cape. Potion choices include moonbeams and stardust. The wands come with gold, copper, or wood handles. The capes come in black, purple, or red. List all the combinations of potions, wand handles, and capes that come in the starter kit.

   Circle 2 kits that cost $25.00.
   Underline 2 kits that cost $10.00.

BRAINWORK: Imagine that you are going to buy a magic carpet from Merlin's shop. You know how much each carpet costs, but will not decide what to buy until you get there. How much money should you bring? Use the information from the price list to explain your answer.

Name: _____ Power Skill: Making a table

All-Star Soccer Stats

It is the end of the regular soccer season, and Coach D. Fence needs to choose 3 players to play in the all-star game. Use the information below to help Coach D. Fence create a table to organize the top players and their statistics. Then analyze the information by answering the questions following the table.

Player #11 had 13 assists, 6 goals, and 19 attempts.
Player #8 had 3 fewer assists than Player #11, the same number of goals as Player #11, and 6 more attempts than Player #11.
The number of assists **Player #24** had matched her player number. She had $\frac{1}{2}$ as many goals and 31 attempts.
Player #15 was the high scorer of the season. She had twice as many goals as Player #24 and the same number of attempts as goals. She had only 9 assists.
Player #1 had twice as many assists and goals as Player #8 and the same number of attempts as assists.
Player #12 had 18 assists, $\frac{1}{2}$ as many goals as assists, and 12 more attempts than Player #1.

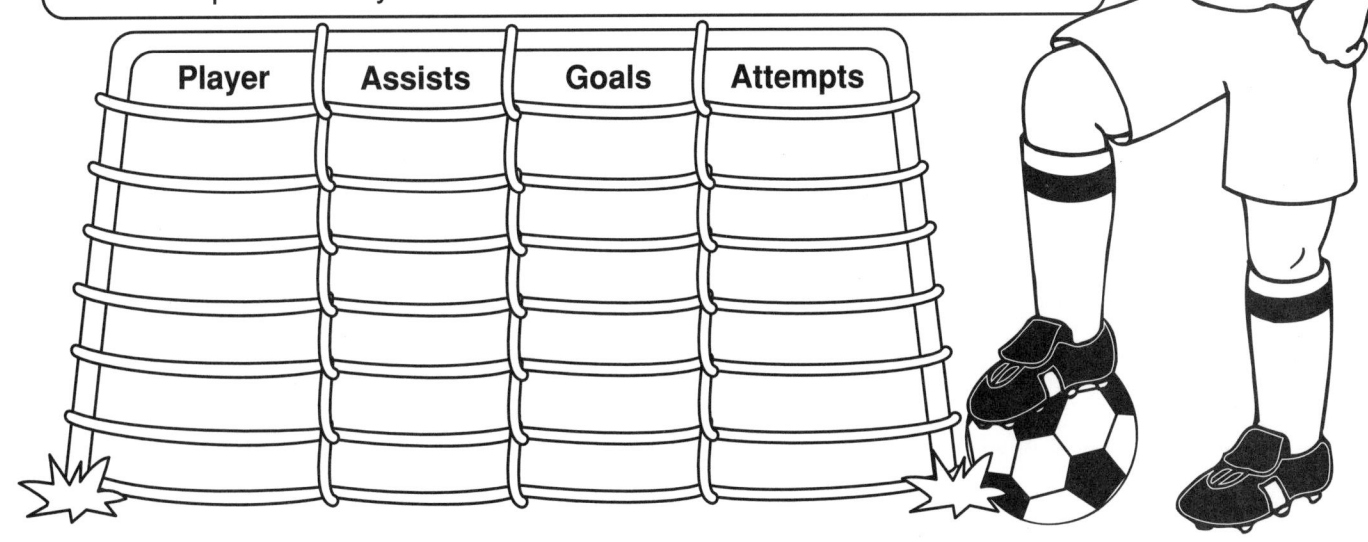

Player	Assists	Goals	Attempts

1. Which player had the greatest number of assists? Goals? Attempts? _____
2. What was the total number of goals scored by these players this season? _____
3. How many more assists than goals did these players have? _____
4. How many more attempts than goals did these players have? _____

BRAINWORK: Which 3 players do you think the coach should send to the all-star game? Why?

Note to the teacher: To make the table more challenging, white-out the headings before making copies.

Name: _____   Power Skill: Making a table

Bubble Gum Bonanza

Don't burst a bubble over these math problems! Each one can be solved by making a table. Complete each table below; then write the solution in the space provided.

1. Jordan chews 3 pieces of gum on Monday, 6 pieces of gum on Tuesday, and 9 pieces of gum on Wednesday. If this pattern continues, how many pieces of gum will Jordan chew on Sunday?
   Solution: _____

Day						
Gum						

2. Jillian's favorite gum flavors are luscious lemon and tangy tangerine. Every 2nd day she chews lemon, and every 3rd day she chews tangerine. How many times will she chew lemon and tangerine on the same day during a 3-week period?
   Solution: _____

Day																					
Lemon																					
Tangerine																					

3. The candy shop at the mall is having a Big Bonanza Bubble Gum Blowout sale. Brandon, the store owner, has decided to give away bubble gum samples. He will give every 3rd person a gumball, every 4th person a stick of gum, and every 6th person a bubble gum sucker. If 30 people visit the shop, how many will receive a gumball and a sucker? How many people will receive all 3?
   Solution: _____

Person	1				5					10					15					20					25					30
Gumball																														
Stick																														
Sucker																														

4. Leonard and Cindy are having a contest to see who can blow the most bubble gum bubbles. Leonard blows 6 bubbles for every 8 bubbles that Cindy blows. If Cindy blows 56 bubbles, how many bubbles will Leonard blow?
   Solution: _____

Leonard							
Cindy							

BRAINWORK: What would the answers be in problem 3 if 60 people visited the shop? Continue the table on the back of this sheet to find the correct answers.

Name: _____

Power Skill: Finding a pattern

Pizza Pie Patterns

Luigi makes pizza pies at the neighborhood pizzeria. Help Luigi solve these problems by identifying the patterns. Write the answer and the pattern for each problem in the corresponding spaces.

1. Luigi can make 2 pepperoni pizza pies using 4 pepperoni sticks, 4 pies using 8 sticks, and 6 pies using 12 sticks. How many sticks will he need to make 10 pies?
   Answer: _____
   Pattern: _____

2. Luigi's sauce requires 15 tomatoes for 3 jars, 20 tomatoes for 4 jars, and 25 tomatoes for 5 jars. How many jars would 50 tomatoes make?
   Answer: _____
   Pattern: _____

3. Luigi made 100 pizza pies on Saturday, 85 on Sunday, 95 on Monday, and 80 on Tuesday. If this trend continues, how many pies will he make on Wednesday?
   Answer: _____
   Pattern: _____

4. Luigi chopped 12 onions and 6 peppers on Wednesday, 11 onions and 5 peppers on Thursday, and 10 onions and 4 peppers on Friday. Following this pattern, how many onions and peppers will he chop on Monday?
   Answer: _____
   Pattern: _____

5. Luigi sells a pizza pack that includes 4 pizza slices, 2 pieces of garlic bread, and 2 drinks. Follow the pattern to complete the table.

Number of Pizza Packs	Included
1	4 slices, 2 pieces, 2 drinks
2	8 slices, 4 pieces, 4 drinks
4	
50	
100	

BRAINWORK: If a family wants a pizza pack with 32 slices of pizza, how many packs should they order? 64 slices? 92 slices?

©2001 The Education Center, Inc. • Power Practice • Math • TEC2667 • Key p. 111

89

Name: _____ **Power Skill:** Finding a pattern

Necklace Number Patterns

Nikki is making a necklace for her new friend, and she needs your help! Help Nikki add color to her necklace by following the directions below.

Directions:
1. Study each number sequence below and discover the pattern.
2. Write each missing number in the appropriate space.
3. Find the rule for each pattern in the necklace at the bottom of the page.
4. Color each bead as indicated in each problem to complete Nikki's necklace.

A. 1, 3, 5, ___, 9, ___, ___, 15, 17, 19, ___ (green)

B. 2, 4, 6, 8, ___, ___, 14, ___, ___, ___, 22 (red)

C. 15, ___, 25, 30, ___, ___, 45, ___, ___ (red)

D. 1, 3, 9, ___, 81, ___, 729, ___, 6,561 (green)

E. 1, 2, 3, 5, 7, 11, ___, 17, ___, 23, 29, ___ (blue)

F. 4, 8, 12, ___, 20, ___, ___, 32, 36, ___, ___ (blue)

G. 2, 8, 6, 12, 10, ___, 14, 20, ___, ___, 22 (green)

H. 7, 9, 8, 10, 9, ___, ___, 12, 11, ___, ___, 14, 13 (yellow)

I. 10, 7, ___, 9, 14, 11, ___, ___, 18, 15, ___, 17, ___, 19 (yellow)

J. 4, 8, 9, 18, ___, ___, 39, ___, ___, 158, 159, ___ (blue)

Beads/rules:
- Even Numbers in Order
- Add 2, Subtract 1
- Multiply by 3
- Odd Numbers in Order
- Multiply by 2, Add 1
- Count by Fives
- Subtract 3, Add 5
- Add 6, Subtract 2
- Prime Numbers in Order
- Add 4

BRAINWORK: On the top part of the back of this sheet, make up 3 new patterns with missing numbers. Then fold the sheet in half and write your answers on the bottom half of the sheet. Ask a friend to solve your patterns.

90 ©2001 The Education Center, Inc. • Power Practice • Math • TEC2667 • Key p. 111

Name: _____

Power Skill: Acting it out

Aquarium Action

Sometimes it's hard to decide how to solve a problem. In some cases, you may find it helpful to act it out. You can use items to represent people or objects. Solve each problem below by acting it out.

1. Mr. C. Otter is taking his class on a field trip to the aquarium. The 1st 5 bus seats are reserved for the adults. Mr. C. Otter sits in the front seat. Mr. B. Ver sits behind Mr. C. Urchin but in front of Mrs. S. Quid. If Mrs. S. H. Ark isn't sitting in the 5th seat, where does she sit? _____

2. In the freshwater tank, a few of the fish have lined up to watch the students pass by. The trout is behind the salmon but in front of the bass. The catfish is in front of the trout but behind the salmon. Which fish is at the front of the line? _____

3. In the saltwater tank, some of the fish have formed a circle. The swordfish is between the mackerel and the marlin. The sailfish is next to the marlin and the sawfish. The tarpon is next to the sawfish but not the sailfish. Which one is between 2 fish with *fish* in their names? _____

4. Sixteen eels are lined up at the front of their tank. As soon as the students start to notice them, they begin to swim back into their caves. First, all the even-numbered eels swim away. Then every 3rd eel of those remaining swims away. Finally, $\frac{1}{2}$ of the remaining eels swim away. How many eels stay at the front of the tank? _____

5. One angelfish is in the middle of a school of fish. There are 13 fish to the right of it. How many total fish are in the school? _____

6. It's feeding time in the shark tank! The white shark gets fed 1st. The nurse shark is fed after the hammerhead shark but before the thresher shark. Which shark is fed last? _____

BRAINWORK: On the back of this sheet, make up your own word problem, using the act-it-out method. Use the ones above as a guide. Then ask a friend to solve it.

©2001 The Education Center, Inc. • *Power Practice • Math* • TEC2667 • Key p. 111

Note to the teacher: Provide students with goldfish-shaped crackers or other counters to complete this activity.

91

Name: _____ Power Skill: Acting it out

Round 'em Up

Rodney Wrangler is trying to round up his herd. Follow the directions below to help Rodney round 'em up!

Directions: Color and cut apart the cards at the bottom of this page. Read the clues for each problem below. Use the cards to act out each solution. Then label the squares to record your arrangement.

1. Each cow has its own pen. Angela and Jessica are next to each other at 1 end. Heather is to the right of Jessica. Hillary is on Angela's right. Gweneth is directly across from Heather. Beverly is next to Gweneth.

2. The cows are standing in 2 rows of 3. Heather is to the right of Angela. Hillary is between Gweneth and Beverly. Angela is above Beverly.

3. The herd has formed a circle. Beverly and Hillary are across from each other. Jessica is between Angela and Beverly. Heather and Gweneth are side by side. Angela is next to Hillary. Gweneth is between Hillary and Heather.

4. Rodney is looking down on the cows from above, and they appear to be standing in a pyramid pattern. Jessica is at the top. Gweneth is between Beverly and Angela. Hillary is diagonally between Jessica and Angela.

BRAINWORK: The herd has lined up to file through the fence to get to the pasture. Hillary is the last one in line. Beverly is behind the first cow in line. Heather is in front of Angela. Gweneth is in front of Heather. Jessica will be the first one to go through the fence. On the back of this sheet, line up and then glue each card in its position in line. Label the first cow in line "first" and the last cow "last."

©2001 The Education Center, Inc. • Power Practice • Math • TEC2667 • Key p. 112

Angela	Beverly	Hillary	Gweneth	Jessica	Heather
Angus	Brahman	Hereford	Guernsey	Jersey	Holstein

92

Name: _____   Power Skill: Drawing a picture

Pat's Party Problems

Pat is having a party! Help her prepare for her party by drawing pictures or diagrams to solve each problem below.

1. Pat's perplexed! Sam wants to sit next to Bill but not Jack. Lee and Bill are left-handed and don't want to bump elbows with Kim, who has a broken arm. Bill and Kim want to sit next to Pat but not Sue. Jan wants to sit next to Jack and across from Sam. Sue wants to sit between Lee and Jack. How should Pat arrange the seats at the table so that everyone is happy?

2. Pat's brother gave her a quarter for her birthday. He told her that he would double her quarter on each of the next 3 days if she didn't spend it. Complete the diagram to find out how much money Pat will have if she waits 3 days.
   _____

3. Pat lined up her 16 presents. The first 12 presents had pink bows on them. The last 9 presents had pink wrapping paper. Label the drawing to show how many presents had both pink bows and pink wrapping paper. _____

4. Pat wants to set up a schedule for a game tournament that starts out with 4 pairs playing and then the winners playing each other until there is only 1 winner left. Each round of the game takes 15 minutes to play, and they will start playing at 1:00. On the back of this sheet, draw a diagram that shows how to organize the rounds and make a schedule that shows how long it will take to play.

5. Pat asked everyone to dress in red and black for her party. Complete the Venn diagram to find out how many were dressed only in red. Out of 8 partygoers, 4 wore red and black. Seven wore red and 5 wore black. How many wore only red? Fill in the Venn diagram to show your answer. _____

BRAINWORK: On another sheet of paper, draw a diagram to represent Pat's 24' x 48' rectangular backyard. Then help Pat set up areas for the following: 12' x 12' eating area, 24' x 12' croquet area, 36' x 12' obstacle course area, and 24' x 12' volleyball area.

©2001 The Education Center, Inc. • Power Practice • Math • TEC2667 • Key p. 112

Name: _____   Power Skill: Drawing a picture

Quads in Squads

The Quinby quadruplets are all on different athletic squads. Help these sporty siblings solve the problems below by drawing a picture on the back of this sheet for each one. Then write your answers in the spaces provided.

1. Robin plays soccer. The soccer field is 200 feet long. Robin's coach told her to kick the ball up and back the length of the field 2 times, up and back $\frac{1}{2}$ of the field 1 time, and then up and back $\frac{1}{4}$ of the field 2 times. How many feet total will Robin have to kick the ball? _____

2. Ross plays baseball. The bases are 60 feet apart. Today, Ross had a great practice. He made it to 2nd base in the 1st inning, he made it to 3rd base in the 3rd inning, and he hit a home run in the last inning. How many feet total did Ross run in practice? _____

3. Rachel is a swimmer. The pool where she swims is 100 feet long and 50 feet wide. Today, Rachel swam twice around the perimeter of the pool. The 1st time she swam the backstroke. The 2nd time she swam the butterfly. How far did Rachel swim the butterfly? What is the total distance she swam?
_____

4. Riley snow-skis. The expert slope at Magic Mountain is 2,000 feet long. The intermediate slope is 800 feet long. Riley skied down the expert slope twice and the intermediate slope 3 times. What is the total distance that Riley skied? _____

5. The Quinby parents have to drive from their house to pick up their kids from each of their activities. They have to drive 60 miles east to pick up Robin, then 20 miles north to pick up Ross, then 60 miles west to pick up Rachel, and then 15 miles north to pick up Riley. At that point, how far are they from home? _____

BRAINWORK: How many total miles do the Quinby parents have to drive to pick up all of their children and get back home? _____ Which child rides the farthest? _____ How far does he or she ride? _____

Name: _____   Power Skill: Understanding algebraic properties

Math Hounds

Sally Stroller is the new dog walker in the neighborhood. To her dismay, she forgot to write down from which property each dog came. Help Sally return each dog to the correct house.

Directions: Read the definition for each *algebraic property* below. Then look at the number sentence shown beneath each dog. Find the house with the matching property. Color the dog the same color as labeled at the top of the house.

Red
Identity Properties

Any number added to zero equals that number.

4 + 0 = 4

Any number multiplied by 1 equals that number.

7 x 1 = 7

Blue
Commutative Property

The order of the addends or factors does not affect the sum or product.

7 + 9 = 9 + 7
3 x 5 = 5 x 3

A. 4 x (5 x 3) = (4 x 5) x 3

B. 8 x (3 + 7) = (8 x 3) + (8 x 7)

C. 34 + 43 = 43 + 34

D. 57 x 1 = 57

E. (24 + 5) + 7 = 24 + (5 + 7)

F. 5 x 26 = (5 x 20) + (5 x 6)

G. 8 + 12 + 3 = 12 + 3 + 8

H. (6 + 12) + 5 = 6 + (12 + 5)

I. 14 + 0 = 14

J. 5 x 14 = 14 x 5

Yellow
Associative Property

Addends or factors can be grouped in any way without changing the sum or product.

(3 + 7) + 5 = 3 + (7 + 5)
5 x (2 x 6) = (5 x 2) x 6

Green
Distributive Property

Multiplying a number by the sum of the addends inside a set of parentheses is the same as multiplying the number by each number inside the parentheses.

4 x (2 + 5) = (4 x 2) + (4 x 5)
8 x 6 = 8 x (3 + 3) = (8 x 3) + (8 x 3)

BRAINWORK: Rewrite and solve each of the following problems using the distributive property: 7 x 6; 13 x 12; 3 x (7 + 2).

Note to the teacher: Provide each student with one copy of this page and colored pencils.

Name: _____   Power Skill: Using algebraic expressions

Boiling Point!

The members of the hit singing group Boiling Point have just launched an exciting Web site! It features math problems related to the band.

Directions: Read each problem. Use the information given in the problem to help you complete the equation. Then solve for *n* and write the answer in the space provided. Be sure to label the units for each answer.

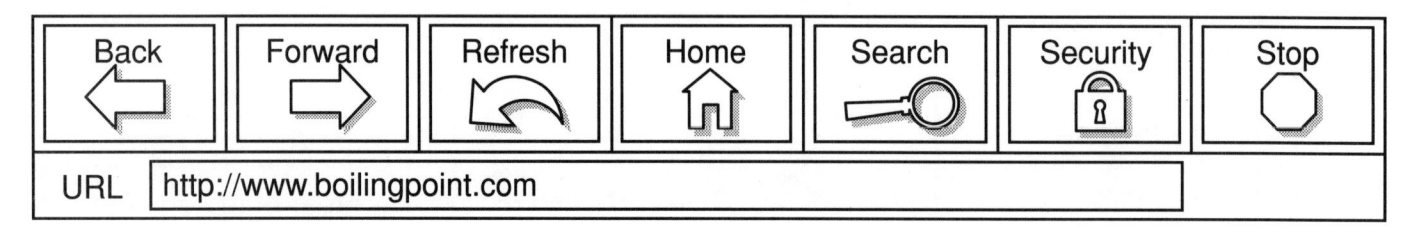

| Back | Forward | Refresh | Home | Search | Security | Stop |

URL | http://www.boilingpoint.com

1. The combined age of all the group members is 98. Jeff is 27 years old. Rick is 26 years old. Jason is 24 years old. How old is Hugh?

    27 + 26 + 24 + n = _____
    Hugh's age _____

2. There are 16 songs on the group's latest CD. The total playing time is 56 minutes. What is the average playing time of each song?

    16n = _____
    Average playing time _____

3. For each practice session last week, Jeff rehearsed for 2 hours. Hugh rehearsed for 1 hour. They rehearsed for a combined total of 36 hours. How long did each group member rehearse in all?

    n + 2n = _____
    Jeff's rehearsal time _____
    Hugh's rehearsal time _____

4. Each of the 4 group members received an equal share of the profits from the group's first CD. The profits totaled $245,624.00. How much did each member receive?

    4n = _____
    Each member's share of the profits _____

6. The group gave 3 concerts last week. Each concert lasted 1 hour longer than the concert before it. All together, the concerts lasted 18 hours. How long was each concert?

    n + (n + 1) + (n + 2) = _____
    1st concert time _____
    2nd concert time _____
    3rd concert time _____

5. Last year, Boiling Point donated $30,000.00 to 2 charities. The group donated $10,000.00 more to Kids for Animals than to Protect the Rain Forests. How much did they donate to each charity?

    n + n + $10,000.00 = _____
    Kids for Animals _____
    Protect the Rain Forests _____

BRAINWORK: The group sold 460,000 CDs in 4 days. On the 1st day, 25,000 CDs were sold. On the 2nd day, 75,000 CDs were sold. Twice as many CDs were sold on the 3rd day than on the 4th day. How many CDs were sold on the 3rd day? Write an equation using *n* to help you solve the problem.

Name: _____   **Power Skill:** Using input/output tables

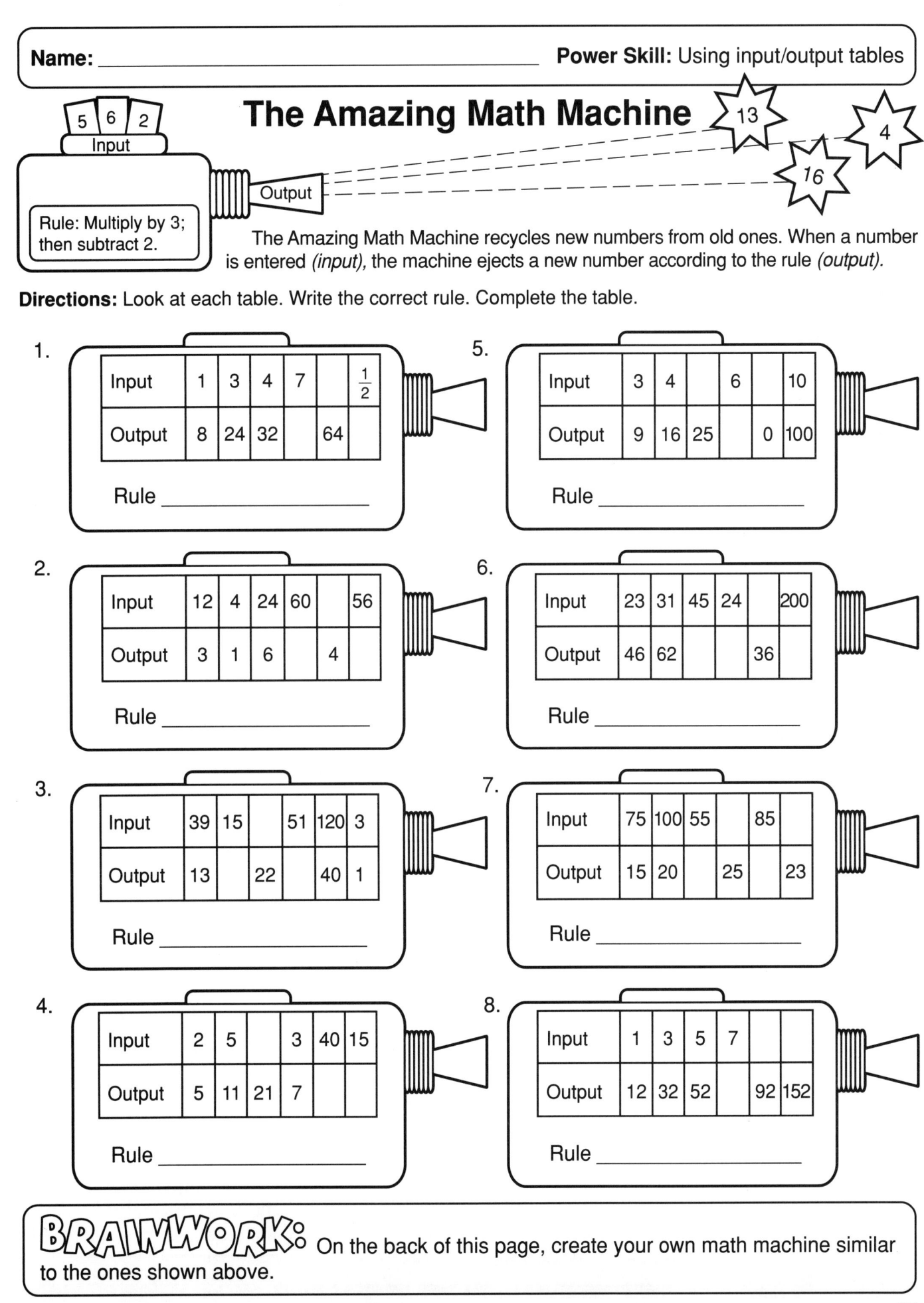

The Amazing Math Machine

Input: 5 6 2
Rule: Multiply by 3; then subtract 2.
Output: 13, 4, 16

The Amazing Math Machine recycles new numbers from old ones. When a number is entered *(input)*, the machine ejects a new number according to the rule *(output)*.

Directions: Look at each table. Write the correct rule. Complete the table.

1.

Input	1	3	4	7	$\frac{1}{2}$
Output	8	24	32		64

Rule _____

2.

Input	12	4	24	60		56
Output	3	1	6		4	

Rule _____

3.

Input	39	15		51	120	3
Output	13		22		40	1

Rule _____

4.

Input	2	5		3	40	15
Output	5	11	21	7		

Rule _____

5.

Input	3	4		6		10
Output	9	16	25		0	100

Rule _____

6.

Input	23	31	45	24		200
Output	46	62			36	

Rule _____

7.

Input	75	100	55		85	
Output	15	20		25		23

Rule _____

8.

Input	1	3	5	7		
Output	12	32	52		92	152

Rule _____

BRAINWORK: On the back of this page, create your own math machine similar to the ones shown above.

Name: _____   Power Skill: Graphing ordered pairs

Readathon

The students at Page Turner Elementary School are holding a Readathon! The students will earn prizes depending on the number of books read.

Directions: Use each algebraic expression to complete each table. Then plot and connect each set of points on the graph below. Trace each line according to the color code.

Grade 3: $x + 2$

x	Books Read	0	1	2	3	4	5
y	Prizes Earned						

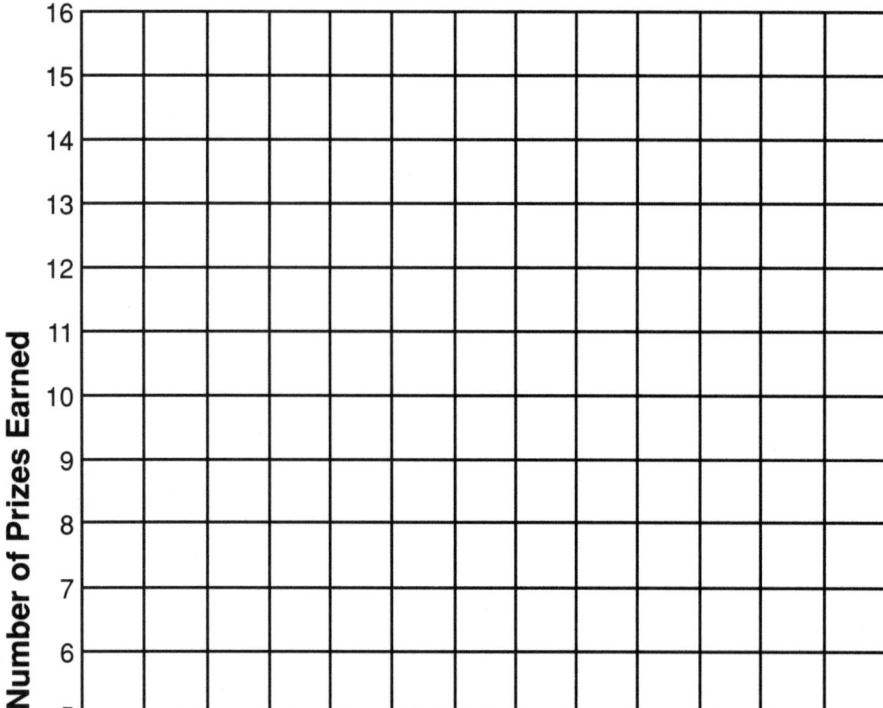

Grade 4: $x - 3$

x	Books Read	3	4	5	6	7	8
y	Prizes Earned						

Grade 5: $\frac{1}{2}x$

x	Books Read	2	4	6	8	10	12
y	Prizes Earned						

Grade 6: $3x$

x	Books Read	0	1	2	3	4	5
y	Prizes Earned						

Color Code
Grade 3 = Red
Grade 4 = Purple
Grade 5 = Blue
Grade 6 = Green

Number of Prizes Earned (y-axis: 0–16)
Number of Books Read (x-axis: 0–13)

BRAINWORK: In which grade can you earn the most prizes for reading the least number of books?

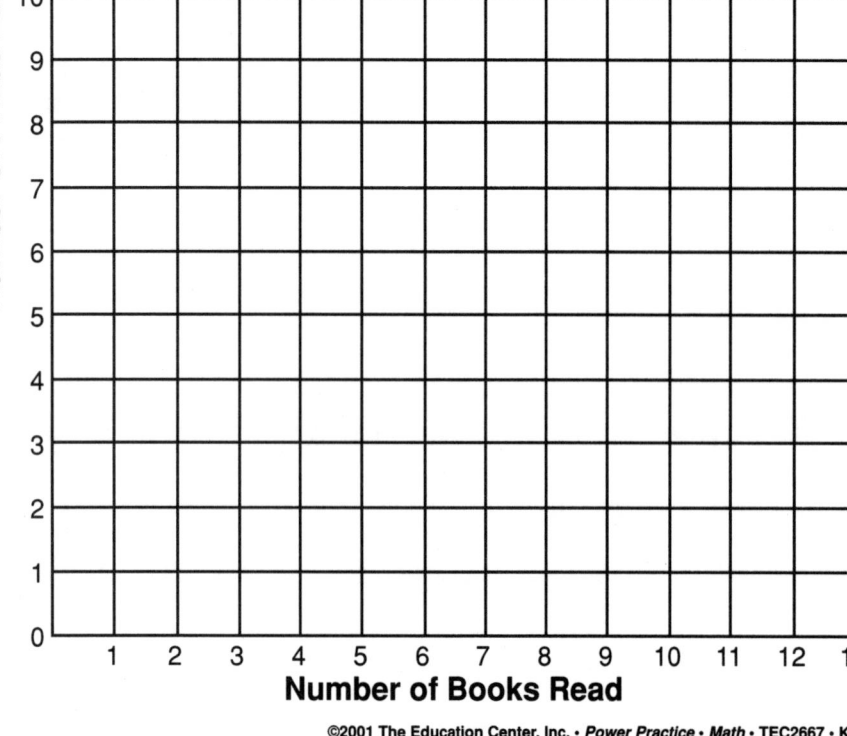

©2001 The Education Center, Inc. • *Power Practice* • *Math* • TEC2667 • Key p. 112

98   **Note to the teacher:** Provide each student with one copy of this page and colored pencils.

Name: _____ **Power Skill:** Finding ordered pairs

Pizza Patterns

Help add pizzazz to these pepperoni pizzas!

Directions: Look at the set of numbered pairs for each pizza. Follow the pattern to complete each chart. Then plot the points on the graph. Finally, connect the points in the order they were plotted to discover the shape the toppings make.

x	y
−2	2
−2	1
	0
	−1
−2	

x	y
−2	−2
−1	−2
1	−2

x	y
2	−2
2	
	0
	1
2	2

x	y
2	2
1	2

(x, y)	(x, y)	(x, y)	(x, y)
(0, 3)	(−3, 0)	(0, −3)	(3, 0)
(−1, 2)	(_, −1)	(1, −2)	(_, _)
(−2, 1)	(−1, _)	(_, _)	(1, 2)
(−3, 0)	(0, −3)	(_, _)	(_, _)

BRAINWORK: Look at the diamond-shaped pizza above. The rule for the line segment that connects (0, 3) and (−3, 0) is subtract 1 for x and subtract 1 for y. Write the rule for the line that connects (−3, 0) and (0, −3).

©2001 The Education Center, Inc. • *Power Practice* • *Math* • TEC2667 • Key p. 112

99

Power Skill: Understanding inequality symbols

Pondering Inequalities

Freddy Frog needs to hop to the other side of the pond. If he hops on a lily pad with the wrong symbol, he will sink to the bottom!

Directions: Look at the number sentence shown on each row of lily pads. Cross out 2 lily pads on each row to make the number sentence correct.

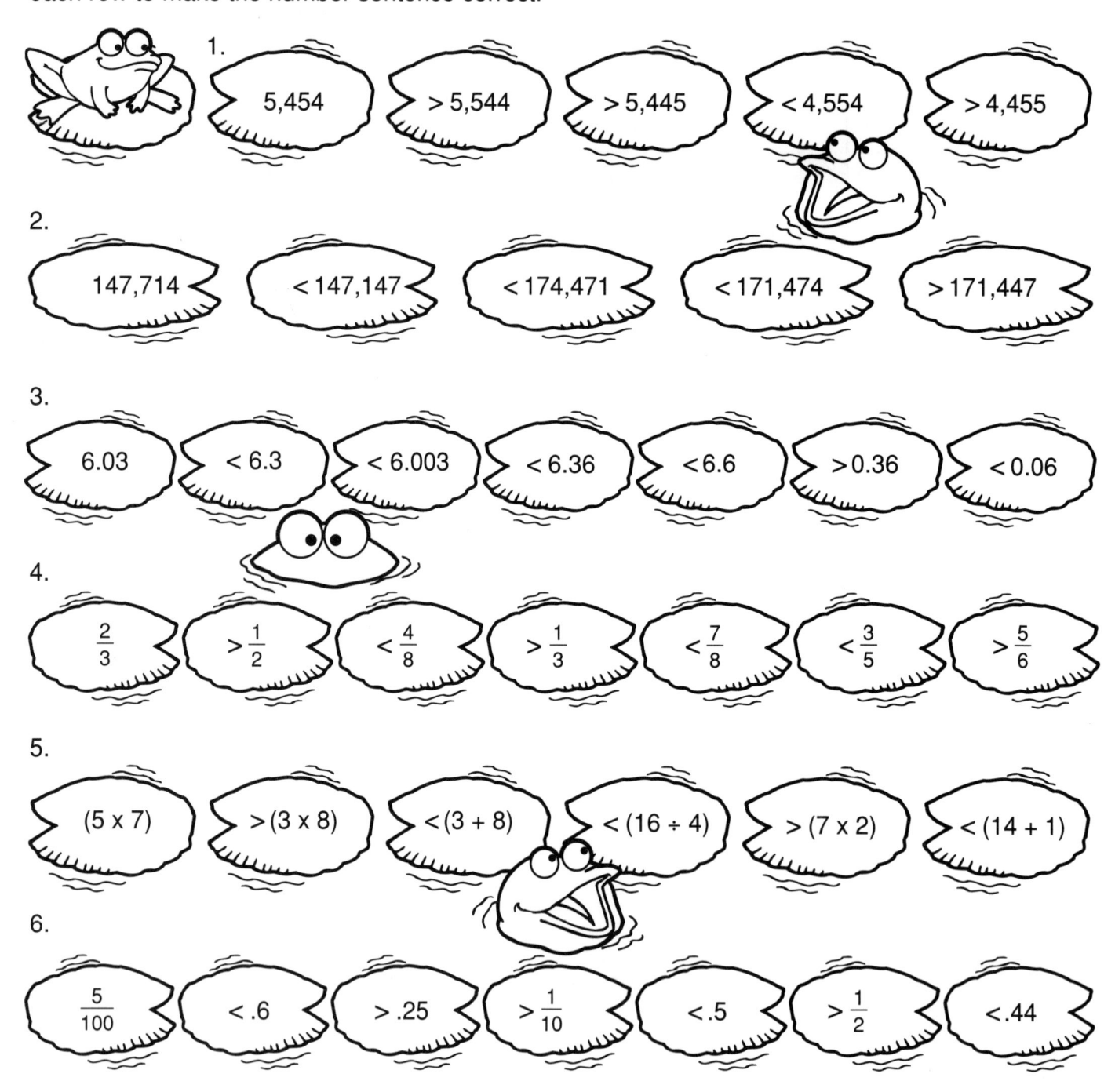

1. 5,454 | > 5,544 | > 5,445 | < 4,554 | > 4,455

2. 147,714 | < 147,147 | < 174,471 | < 171,474 | > 171,447

3. 6.03 | < 6.3 | < 6.003 | < 6.36 | < 6.6 | > 0.36 | < 0.06

4. $\frac{2}{3}$ | $> \frac{1}{2}$ | $< \frac{4}{8}$ | $> \frac{1}{3}$ | $< \frac{7}{8}$ | $< \frac{3}{5}$ | $> \frac{5}{6}$

5. (5 × 7) | > (3 × 8) | < (3 + 8) | < (16 ÷ 4) | > (7 × 2) | < (14 + 1)

6. $\frac{5}{100}$ | < .6 | > .25 | $> \frac{1}{10}$ | < .5 | $> \frac{1}{2}$ | < .44

BRAINWORK: On the back of this page, draw a row of lily pads. Write a 5-digit number on each lily pad. Write the correct inequality symbol between each pair of lily pads.

Name: _____ Power Skill: Finding addends and factors

Alphabet Cereal Algebra

Alfie spilled his alphabet cereal all over his math homework! Each cereal letter is covering a number in a math problem. Solve each equation below to reveal the hidden number.

Name: **Alfie** Math Homework

1. $50 + f = 83$

    f = ___

2. $o + 999 = 1{,}004$

    o = ___

3. $867 - k = 49$

    k = ___

4. $103 + s = 206$

    s = ___

5. $e + 2{,}727 = 3{,}000$

    e = ___

6. $563 \times r = 2{,}252$

    r = ___

7. $l \times 11 = 110$

    l = ___

8. $18 \times 14 = n$

    n = ___

9. $22 \times a = 4{,}180$

    a = ___

10. $c \times 95 = 570$

    c = ___

BRAINWORK: Rearrange the alphabet letters to spell a crow's favorite cereal.

Name: _____   Power Skill: Writing equations

Challenging the Peaks

Melinda needs to know the distance up and down each mountain shown below to plan her biking trip. She'll begin at Mt. Peak and end at the bottom of Mt. Low. Follow the directions below to help her determine each distance.

Directions:
1. Look at the map.
2. For each clue, underline the distance that you are trying to find.
3. Write an equation. Use *x* to represent the unknown distance.
4. Solve the equation.
5. Label the distance on the map. The first one has been done for you.

Clue 1: The distance <u>up Mt. Peak</u> is half the distance up Mt. High Point.

Equation: $x = \frac{1}{2}(6)$
             $x = 3$

Clue 2: The distance up Mt. Steep is twice as long as the distance up Mt. Peak.

Equation: _____

Clue 3: The distance down Mt. Peak and up Mt. Steep is the same as the distance down Mt. Grande and up Mt. High Point.

Equation: _____

Clue 4: The distance up and down Mt. Steep is the same distance down Mt. High Point.

Equation: _____

Clue 5: The distance up and down Mt. Low is the same distance down Mt. High Point.

Equation: _____

Clue 6: The total distance up and down all the mountains is 82 miles. Find the distance up Mt. Grande.

Equation: _____

BRAINWORK: Melinda completed her biking trip in 123 hours, excluding rest time. On average, how many miles per hour did she travel?

Name: _____   Power Skill: Calculating integers

Icy Cold Integers

Help the weather station's forecaster, I. C. Cold, predict the temperature. Read each problem. Write the new temperature on the blank provided. Remember to label your answers in °C.

1. It is 15°C. It will be 25° colder by midnight.

   Temperature at midnight _____

2. The overnight low was –12°C. The temperature is expected to rise 15° by noon.

   Temperature at noon _____

3. The present temperature is –1°C. It will drop 19° by lunchtime.

   Temperature at lunchtime _____

4. The temperature dropped 17° at 3:00 P.M. from 4°C.

   Temperature at 3:00 P.M. _____

5. It is now –4°C. The temperature is expected to rise 33° by Sunday.

   Temperature on Sunday _____

6. Yesterday's temperature was 24°C. Today's temperature was 5° colder than yesterday. Tomorrow's temperature will be 20° colder than today.

   Tomorrow's temperature _____

7. The temperature was 8°C on Monday. It dropped 2° every day for the rest of the week.

   Temperature on Saturday _____

8. The temperature was 16°C at noon. It dropped 20° 2 hours later. Then it rose 15° 3 hours later.

   Temperature at 2:00 P.M. _____
   Temperature at 5:00 P.M. _____

9. The temperature on Thursday was –5°C. The temperature was twice as high the following day.

   Temperature on Friday _____

10. The temperature was 8°C today, which was 15° warmer than yesterday.

    Yesterday's temperature _____

BRAINWORK: Water freezes at 0°C. Fill in the thermometer above to show one possible temperature for a snowy day. Explain your answer on the back of this page.

Answer Keys

Page 4
Answers may vary. Accept reasonable responses.
1. 633
2. 6,321
3. 676,676
4. 36,421
5. 936
6. 2,663

Page 5
1. correct
2. correct
3. incorrect
4. incorrect
5. correct
6. correct
7. incorrect
8. correct
9. correct
10. correct
11. incorrect
12. incorrect
13. incorrect
14. correct
15. correct
16. incorrect
17. correct
18. incorrect
19. correct
20. correct
21. incorrect

The ancient number system is Egyptian hieroglyphics.

BRAINWORK: Answers will vary, but students should list 5 facts about Egyptian hieroglyphics.

Page 6
Left wing:
8,210 = 8,210
13,002 < 13,071
12,098 > 11,089
5,041 < 5,319
11,342 > 10,342
21,129 = 21,129
41,131 = 41,131
24,422 > 24,420
2,496 < 2,946
98,701 = 98,701
310,601 = 310,601
930 < 932
2,916 > 2,910
8,808 < 18,808
27,216 > 15,516
3,904 = 3,904
2,112 < 11,121
741 > 147
10,000 < 10,010
4,663 > 2,598
8,716 < 9,831
711 = 711
4,117 = 4,117
3,743 < 3,842
721 > 271

Right wing:
64,679 = 64,679
12,339 > 11,239
3,743 < 3,842
82,100 > 81,200
470,360 < 470,368
7,468 = 7,468
17,395 = 17,395
1,553 < 3,221
71,814 > 17,757
42,100 = 42,100
14,733 = 14,733
5,015 > 5,005
8,486 < 11,783
1,231 > 999
4,211 < 5,724
985 = 985
18,011 < 18,110
39,087 < 39,188
723 > 237
7,560 < 7,712
9,000 > 900
6,980 = 6,980
5,322 = 5,322
46,215 > 43,789
345,011 < 345,101

BRAINWORK:
147	1,231	10,342	24,420
237	2,598	11,089	24,422
271	2,910	11,239	27,216
721	2,916	11,342	43,789
723	4,663	12,098	46,215
741	5,005	12,339	71,814
900	5,015	15,516	81,200
999	9,000	17,757	82,100

Page 7

100-Meter Backstroke
Place	Lane	Time
1st	4	54.66
2nd	5	54.75
3rd	1	55.12
4th	3	55.39
5th	2	55.45

100-Meter Freestyle
Place	Lane	Time
1st	1	48.52
2nd	4	48.59
3rd	3	48.95
4th	5	49.01
5th	2	49.10

100-Meter Butterfly
Place	Lane	Time
1st	3	53.14
2nd	1	53.19
3rd	4	53.23
4th	5	53.32
5th	2	53.56

BRAINWORK: <, >, >

Page 8
1st Alien: 15, 21, 33
2nd Alien: 2, 13, 37
3rd Alien: 25, 49, 100
4th Alien: 18, 24, 42
5th Alien: 9, 45, 63

BRAINWORK: 2, 3, 5, 7, 11, 13, 17, 19, 23, 29, 31, 37, 41, 43, 47

Page 9
1. french fry
2. burger
3. burger
4. burger
5. french fry
6. french fry
7. burger or french fry
8. lettuce
9. tomato
10. carrot (It depends on whether the negative or positive number is larger.)
11. tomato
12. lettuce
13. tomato
14. carrot
15. lettuce

BRAINWORK: depth below ground = −3; ground level = 0; height above ground = 4 or +4

Page 10
1. +12
2. −6
3. +4
4. +10
5. +9
6. +4
7. +9
8. −5
9. +11
10. +12

BRAINWORK:
Tigers +43 yards
Lions +17 yards
The Tigers gained the most yardage in the second half of the game.

Page 11
1. −4, −3, 0, +7
2. −10, 0, +2, +3
3. −14, −6, 0, +1
4. −13, −5, +5, +12
5. −11, −9, +4, +20
6. −15, −8, +11, +19
7. −41, −21, +40, +65
8. −98, +95, +99, +100

BRAINWORK: the Chance house

Page 12
Dinah's Collection
5 WN, I, F, D
$2/4$ F, D
−8 I, F, D
$13/39$ F, D
−6 I, F, D
235 WN, I, F, D
$5^1/8$ F, D
$1/7$ F, D
7.36 F, D

Armand's Collection
2.75 F, D
$2/6$ F, D
78 WN, I, F, D
$3^5/6$ F, D
$13/14$ F, D
40 WN, I, F, D
−90 I, F, D
$5^4/5$ F, D
$7/8$ F, D

Sid's Collection
6.9 F, D
−18 I, F, D
$6/18$ F, D
$32^1/5$ F, D
70 WN, I, F, D
−11.3 F, D
$3^3/11$ F, D
11.77 F, D
$1/5$ F, D
54 WN, I, F, D

Imogene's Collection
$3^1/3$ F, D
$3/1$ WN, I, F, D
30 WN, I, F, D
$6^1/3$ F, D
4.77 F, D
−53 I, F, D
$12^4/5$ F, D
5.7 F, D
77.88 F, D

BRAINWORK: Answers will vary.

Page 13
Popcorn: $1/3$, $2/3$, 0.75, $8/9$, $8/7$, 3, 3.2, $3^2/3$
Caramel Corn: $1/5$, 0.25, 0.5, $2/3$, 1.12, 1.25, $4/3$, $1^1/2$
BRAINWORK: Answers will vary.

Page 14
1. 64
2. 400
3. 100
4. 121
5. 225
6. 361
7. 961
8. 625
9. 100
10. 400

1. 7
2. 10
3. 9
4. 1
5. 20
6. 30
7. 24
8. 80
9. 100
10. 10
11. 4
12. 10

Riddle 1: FOUR SQUARE
Riddle 2: YOU'RE PERFECT!

BRAINWORK: 14 (1, 4, 9, 16, 25, 36, 49, 64, 81, 100, 121, 144, 169, 196)

Page 15
1. $94,742
2. $283,963
3. $276,354
4. $323,610
5. $247,070
6. $155,214
7. $624,222
8. $56,796

BRAINWORK: $2,062,000

Page 16
Aug. 1—Beginning mileage: 81,151
Mileage for the day: 1,068
Aug. 4—From: Atlanta
Mileage for the day: 256
Aug. 6—To: Seattle
Beginning mileage: 82,475
Mileage for the day: 2,512
Aug. 8—Ending mileage: 87,743
Mileage for the day: 2,756
Aug. 10—To: Nashville
Beginning mileage: 87,743
Mileage for the day: 256
Aug. 12—From: Nashville
Beginning mileage: 87,999
Ending mileage: 88,782
Mileage for the day: 783
Aug. 14—To: Boston
Mileage for the day: 1,916

BRAINWORK: 9,547 miles, 453 more miles

Page 17
1. 148
2. 61
3. 7,398
4. 241
5. 1,474
6. 2,953
7. 2,882
8. 2,563

A suburban submarine!

BRAINWORK: Answers will vary.

Page 18
Part 1
1. Laurie: 22 + 25 + 50 + 18 = about 120 tickets
2. Sammy: 75 + 50 + 11 + 33 = about 170 tickets
3. Francesca: 25 + 35 + 75 + 10 = about 160 tickets
4. Jessica: 33 + 20 + 18 + 25 = about 100 tickets
5. Dylan: 10 + 50 + 14 + 33 = about 100 tickets
6. Nick: 22 + 18 + 50 + 33 = about 120 tickets

Jillian will need about 770 total tickets.

Part 2
Jillian will need about $39.00.

BRAINWORK: Answers will vary.

Page 20
1. 436 bubbles x 484 uses = 211,024 bubbles
2. 436 bubbles x 149 uses = 64,964 bubbles
3. 738 bubbles x 752 uses = 554,976 bubbles
4. 738 bubbles x 841 uses = 620,658 bubbles
5. 947 bubbles x 236 uses = 223,492 bubbles
6. 947 bubbles x 542 uses = 513,274 bubbles
7. 947 bubbles x 560 uses = 530,320 bubbles
8. 963 bubbles x 317 uses = 305,271 bubbles

BRAINWORK: Answers will vary. Based on the data, none of the wands will produce billions of bubbles in an hour.

Page 19
1. 1,872
2. 3,825
3. 8,464
4. 3,432
5. 5,264
6. 5,082
7. 4,784
8. 4,770
9. 4,137
10. 2,870
11. 9,889
12. 5,700

BRAINWORK: 8,100 inches

Page 21
W 430
N 74
G 144
E 487
L 404
A 964
I 485
G 600
L 361
A 24
L 42
R 104
T 314
A 98
T 248
A 466
C 649
P 279
O 435
H 417
H 542
E 44
F 743
M 237
T 58

The Great Wall of China

BRAINWORK: 500, 6

Page 22
1. 3 r5
2. 9 r4
3. 12 r1
4. 6 r10
5. 4 r11
6. 8 r7
7. 3 r9
8. 16 r2
9. 4 r22
10. 6 r8
11. 15 r3
12. 3 r19
13. 4 r14
14. 4 r20
15. 5 r17
16. 8 r6

BRAINWORK: approximately 273 days

Page 23
1. Estimate: 3, Exact: 3 r1, Total: 4
2. Estimate: 8, Exact: 8 r37, Total: 9
3. Estimate: 6, Exact: 6 r31, Total: 7
4. Estimate: 55, Exact: 55 r7, Total: 56
5. Estimate: 45, Exact: 45 r10, Total: 46
6. Estimate: 2, Exact: 2 r6, Total: 3
7. Estimate: 4, Exact: 4 r1, Total: 5
8. Estimate: 15, Exact: 15 r6, Total: 16
9. Estimate: 140, Exact: 143 r5, Total: 144
10. Estimate: 80, Exact: 86 r7, Total: 87
11. Estimate: 200, Exact: 216 r1, Total: 217
12. Estimate: 60, Exact: 62, Total: 62
13. Estimate: 8, Exact: 8 r7, Total: 9
14. Estimate: 11, Exact: 11 r43, Total: 12

BRAINWORK: 677 boxes

Page 24
The following sets of flags should be colored the same:
$1/2$, 0.5, 50%
$1/4$, 0.25, 25%
$5/8$, 0.625, 62.5%
$3/4$, 0.75, 75%
$2/5$, 0.4, 40%
$11/20$, 0.55, 55%
$18/100$, 0.18, 18%
$7/10$, 0.7, 70%
$1/5$, 0.2, 20%
$3/50$, 0.06, 6%

BRAINWORK: Answers will vary.

Page 25
1. $3/5$
2. $5/6$
3. $6/7$
4. $3/4$
5. $6/9 = 2/3$
6. $5/8$
7. $8/6 = 1\,1/3$
8. $6/4 = 1\,1/2$
9. $11/8 = 1\,3/8$
10. $8/5 = 1\,3/5$
11. $9/9 = 1$
12. $10/6 = 1\,2/3$

BOO-BERRY PIE WITH I-SCREAM!

BRAINWORK: Answers will vary.

105

Page 26
A. 13$\frac{1}{3}$
B. 10$\frac{4}{5}$
C. 9$\frac{1}{2}$
D. 12$\frac{2}{3}$
E. 8$\frac{1}{4}$
F. 7$\frac{1}{2}$
G. 7$\frac{1}{3}$
H. 11
I. 18$\frac{4}{5}$
J. 4$\frac{2}{3}$
K. 7$\frac{1}{5}$
L. 15
M. 12$\frac{2}{5}$
N. 8$\frac{2}{3}$
O. 13$\frac{2}{3}$
P. 18

BRAINWORK: 8$\frac{1}{6}$

Page 27
2. $\frac{6}{6} - \frac{2}{6} = \frac{4}{6}$
$\frac{4}{6} - \frac{1}{6} = \frac{3}{6}$
$\frac{3}{6} - \frac{2}{6} = \frac{1}{6}$
Fractional amount left: $\frac{1}{6}$

3. $\frac{10}{10} - \frac{3}{10} = \frac{7}{10}$
$\frac{7}{10} - \frac{1}{10} = \frac{6}{10}$
$\frac{6}{10} - \frac{4}{10} = \frac{2}{10}$
Fractional amount left: $\frac{1}{5}$

4. $\frac{9}{9} - \frac{3}{9} = \frac{6}{9}$
$\frac{6}{9} - \frac{2}{9} = \frac{4}{9}$
$\frac{4}{9} - \frac{1}{9} = \frac{3}{9}$
Fractional amount left: $\frac{1}{3}$

5. $\frac{12}{12} - \frac{1}{12} = \frac{11}{12}$
$\frac{11}{12} - \frac{3}{12} = \frac{8}{12}$
$\frac{8}{12} - \frac{2}{12} = \frac{6}{12}$
Fractional amount left: $\frac{1}{2}$

6. $\frac{16}{16} - \frac{3}{16} = \frac{13}{16}$
$\frac{13}{16} - \frac{5}{16} = \frac{8}{16}$
$\frac{8}{16} - \frac{6}{16} = \frac{2}{16}$
Fractional amount left: $\frac{1}{8}$

BRAINWORK: $\frac{1}{8}$, $\frac{1}{6}$, $\frac{1}{5}$, $\frac{1}{4}$, $\frac{1}{3}$, $\frac{1}{2}$

Page 28
2. $\frac{4}{15}$
3. $\frac{5}{18}$
4. $\frac{3}{20}$
5. $\frac{2}{10} = \frac{1}{5}$
6. $\frac{15}{30} = \frac{1}{2}$
7. $\frac{9}{20}$
8. $\frac{3}{16}$
9. $\frac{8}{24} = \frac{1}{3}$
10. $\frac{4}{27}$

BRAINWORK:

Y	Y	Y	Y	Y			
RY	RY	RY	RY	RY	R	R	R
RY	RY	RY	RY	RY	R	R	R
RY	RY	RY	RY	RY	R	R	R

Page 29
1. blue $\frac{3}{4}$
   black 1
   white $\frac{4}{5}$
2. red $\frac{1}{2}$
   white $\frac{4}{5}$
   blue $\frac{3}{4}$
3. yellow 1$\frac{1}{2}$
   blue $\frac{3}{4}$
   red $\frac{1}{2}$
4. green 2
   yellow 1$\frac{1}{2}$
   red $\frac{1}{2}$

5. white $\frac{4}{5}$
   green 2
   red $\frac{1}{2}$
6. red $\frac{1}{2}$
   white $\frac{4}{5}$
   black 1
7. green 2
   white $\frac{4}{5}$
   blue $\frac{3}{4}$
8. red $\frac{1}{2}$
   white $\frac{4}{5}$
   green 2

BRAINWORK: Answers will vary.

Page 30
1. $4.29 + $3.33 + $3.88 = $11.50 − $1.00 = $10.50
2. $2.77 + $4.29 + $3.89 = $10.95 + $2.25 = $13.20
3. $3.89 + $3.33 + $4.29 + $3.88 = $15.39 − $3.33 = $12.06 + $4.50 (2 x $2.25) = $16.56
4. $2.77 + $3.89 = $6.66 − $1.50 (2 x $0.75) = $5.16
5. $2.77 + $3.75 + $3.75 = $10.27 − $1.00 = $9.27
6. $3.75 + $2.77 + $3.33 + $2.77 = $12.62 − $2.77 = $9.85 + $2.25 = $12.10
7. $2.77 + $3.88 + $2.77 = $9.42

BRAINWORK: Answers will vary.

Page 31
A. 0.06 (2 decimal places)
B. 0.246 (3 decimal places)
C. 1.2 (1 decimal place)
D. 2.162 (3 decimal places)
E. 0.0036 (4 decimal places)
F. 107.1 (1 decimal place)
G. 2.94 (2 decimal places)
H. 0.25 (2 decimal places)
I. 7.21 (2 decimal places)
J. 0.063 (3 decimal places)
K. 0.0588 (4 decimal places)
L. 12.6 (1 decimal place)

Mugsy's bone is buried in hole G.

BRAINWORK: A x B = 0.01476, C x D = 2.5944, E x F = 0.38556, G x H = 0.735, I x J = 0.45423, and K x L = 0.74088

Page 32
A. 0.6
B. 0.21
C. 0.5
D. 9.08
E. 5.15
F. 0.05
G. 3.95
H. 5.38
I. 13.2

BRAINWORK: 0.037

Page 33
Answers will vary.

BRAINWORK:
Parallel lines: E, F, H, I, M, N, Z
Perpendicular lines: E, F, H, I, L, T

Page 34
Acute angles: 1, 2, 7, 15
Right angles: 3, 5, 6, 8, 10, 12
Obtuse angles: 4, 9, 11, 13, 14

BRAINWORK: Answers will vary.

Page 35
Trudy = green
Octavia = orange
Penny = purple
Hector = yellow
Mrs. Polygon = red
Mr. Polygon = blue

BRAINWORK: Answers will vary.

Page 36
red: O, K, Y, P, E
blue: Q, B, R
yellow: M, N, U, S
green: A, G
orange: J, D
Terra Turtle's bathing suit is "pokey-dot."

BRAINWORK: Answers will vary.

Page 37

(Triangle classification diagram with triangles labeled: Equilateral, Scalene, Scalene, Right, Isosceles, Scalene, Isosceles, Equilateral, Scalene, Isosceles, Equilateral, Isosceles, Right, Right, Equilateral, Scalene)

Page 38
1. cube
2. sphere
3. rectangular solid
4. cone
5. cylinder
6. pyramid

Page 39
Similar polygons (yellow)
    When—end
    By—never
    every—go
    all—reads
    arm—skin
    a—hole
    always—in
Congruent polygons (green)
    The—can
    If—after
    while—books
    slides—home
    Riddle: Because you can't pull his leg!

Page 41

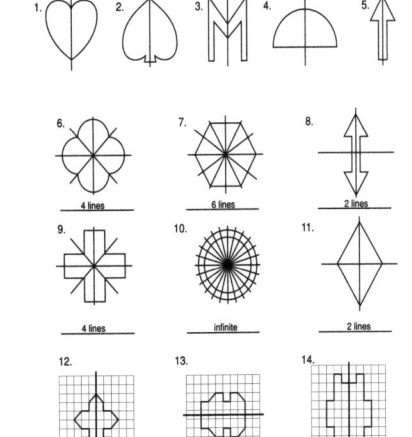

(Lines of symmetry figures: 1–5 single figures; 6. 4 lines; 7. 6 lines; 8. 2 lines; 9. 4 lines; 10. infinite; 11. 2 lines; 12–14. grid figures with symmetry lines)

Page 42
Part I:
1. reflection, Flip-a-figure
2. rotation, Turn-a-lily
3. translation, Slide-a-mid
4. translation, Slide-a-pillar
5. rotation, Turn-a-ball
6. reflection, Flip-o-saur

Part II: Answers will vary.

Page 43
Guion
grades
trained
aerospace
aircraft
earned
Astronaut
space

BRAINWORK: *Challenger*

Page 44

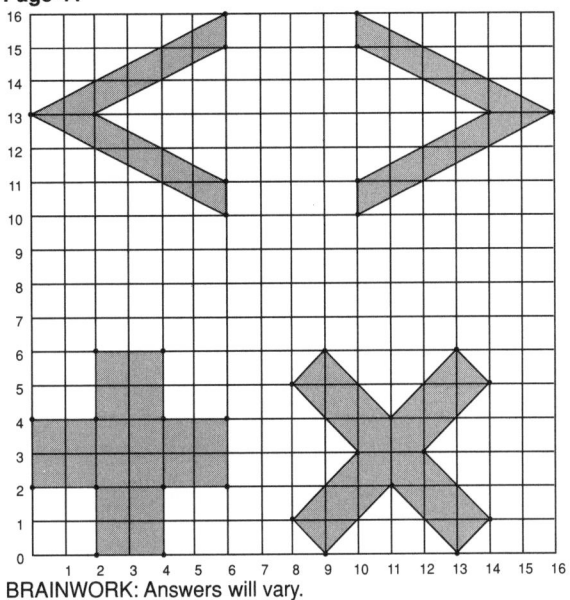

(Coordinate grid with shaded figures)

BRAINWORK: Answers will vary.

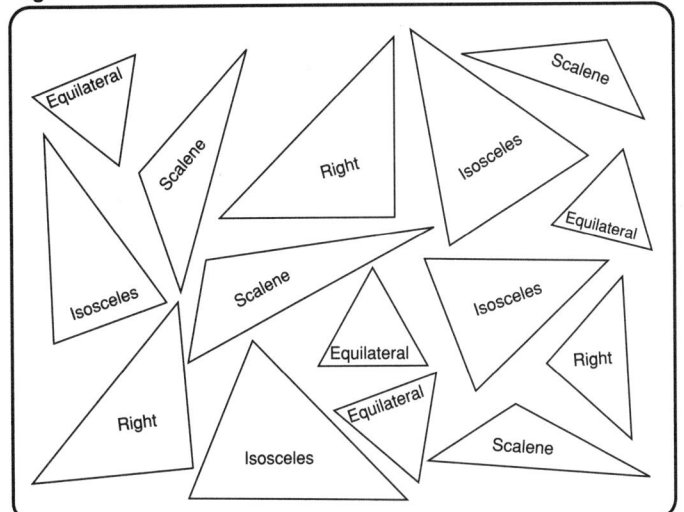

Page 46
Drawings will vary but should accurately reflect the radius and diameter measurements given.

BRAINWORK:
1. 6.28 cm
2. 62.8 mm
3. 94.2 mm
4. 157 mm
5. 31.4 mm
6. 12.56 cm
7. 6.28 cm
8. 31.4 mm
9. 12.56 cm

Page 47

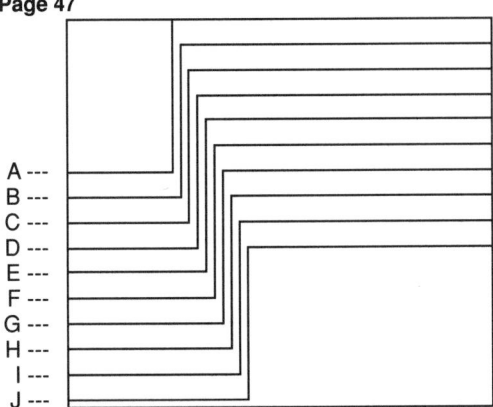

(Illustration of lines A–J)

Depending on the way you look at it, either side can appear higher.

BRAINWORK: The lines are the same length. The second line appears longer because the lines on the ends seem to make the line expand.

107

Page 48
1. $5^{1}/_{2}$"
2. $3^{1}/_{2}$"
3. $1^{1}/_{4}$"
4. $1^{3}/_{4}$"
5. $1^{3}/_{4}$"
6. $^{1}/_{2}$"
7. $1^{1}/_{8}$"
8. $1^{3}/_{8}$"
9. $^{6}/_{8}$" = $^{3}/_{4}$"
10. $^{3}/_{16}$"
11. $^{5}/_{16}$"
12. $^{13}/_{16}$"
13. $^{7}/_{16}$"
14. $^{8}/_{16}$" = $^{1}/_{2}$"
15. $^{2}/_{16}$" = $^{1}/_{8}$"

Page 49
1. 3 cm
2. 2 cm
3. 4 cm
4. 5 cm
5. 7 cm
6. 70 mm
7. 50 mm
8. 30 mm
9. 40 mm
10. 20 mm

Matches: 1 and 8, 2 and 10, 3 and 9, 4 and 7, 5 and 6

BRAINWORK: millipedes 210 mm, 21 cm; centipedes 21 cm, 210 mm

Page 50
1. km
2. m
3. kl
4. g
5. l
6. kg
7. m
8. dal
9. hg
10. cm
11. cl
12. mg
13. kg
14. m

Page 51
1. 3 oz.
2. 5 lb.
3. 12 oz.
4. 55 lb.
5. 3 T

6. 1 gal., 2 qt.
7. 1 gal., 1 pt.
8. 1 gal., $^{3}/_{4}$ gal.
9. 1 gal., $^{1}/_{2}$ gal.
10. 1 gal., 4 pt.

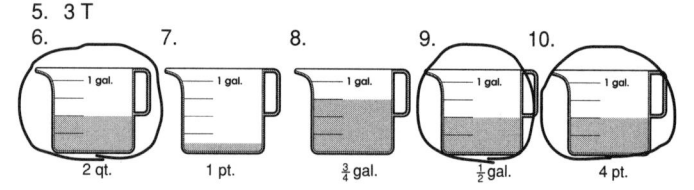

11. 2 c., 1 pt.
12. $^{1}/_{2}$ gal., 2 qt.
13. 3 qt.
14. 1 gal., 8 pt., 4 qt.
15. 1 qt.

BRAINWORK: Lists will vary but should include the most reasonable unit of measure that would be used to measure each item.

Page 52
1. 50°F
2. 30°F
3. 86°F
4. 62°F
5. 73°F
6. 82°F
7. 78°F
8. 29°F
9. 35°F
10. 73°F

Page 53

City	Celsius Temperature	Fahrenheit Temperature	City	Celsius Temperature	Fahrenheit Temperature
London	4°C	39°F	Madrid	9°C	48°F
Paris	15°C	59°F	Oslo	0°C	32°F
Athens	10°C	50°F	Berlin	18°C	64°F
Zurich	22°C	72°F	Lisbon	12°C	54°F
Rome	13°C	55°F	Dublin	7°C	45°F

1. 11°C, 20°F
2. 3°C, 6°F
3. 10°C, 18°F
4. 5°C, 9°F
5. 13°C
6. 21°F

BRAINWORK: Responses should include today's high and low in your town in degrees Celsius and Fahrenheit.

108

Page 54
1. 56 min., 4th
2. 1 hr., 5th
3. 53 min., 3rd
4. 1 hr. 13 min., 7th
5. 49 min., 2nd
6. 1 hr. 21 min., 9th
7. 47 min., 1st
8. 1 hr. 8 min., 6th
9. 1 hr. 16 min., 8th
10. 1 hr. 22 min., 10th
11. 2 hr. 52 min.
12. 1 hr. 55 min.

BRAINWORK: Responses will vary but should list the times they wake up, go to school, get home, and go to bed as well as the elapsed time between waking up and going to school, waking up and getting home, and waking up and going to bed.

Page 55
1. 50 ft.^{2}
2. 9 m^2
3. 120,000 cm^2
4. 24 m^2
5. 4.5 ft.^{2}
6. 12 ft.^{2}
7. 14 ft.^{2}
8. 21 m^2
9. 10.24 m^2
10. 32 ft.^{2}
11. 80,000 cm^2
12. 1,470,000 cm^2

BRAINWORK: Hannah's garden is 21 m^2, or 2,100 cm^2. Carrie's garden is 80,000 cm^2. Carrie's garden is larger; students should have shaded the triangle in problem 11.

Page 56
Bowzer: A. 11.5 cm^2, B. 11 cm^2, C. 20 cm^2; C gives Bowzer the most space.
Buddy: A. 13.5 in.^{2}, B. 17.5 in.^{2}, C. 24.5 in.^{2}; C gives Buddy the most space.
Boomer: A. 28.5 x 5 cm^2 = 142.5 cm^2, B. 10 x 5 cm^2 = 50 cm^2, C. 27 x 5 cm^2 = 135 cm^2; A gives Boomer the most space.

BRAINWORK: Drawings for Beamer's new space will vary.

Page 57
1. 18 yd.
2. 16 yd.
3. 32 yd.
4. 10.5 cm x 5 yd. = 52.5 yd.
5. 9 cm x 5 yd. = 45 yd.
6. 10 cm x 5 yd. = 50 yd.
7. 11 cm x 12 yd. = 132 yd.
8. 12 cm x 12 yd. = 144 yd.
9. 15 cm x 12 yd. = 180 yd.

A. Two possible perimeters are 22 yd. for a 2 x 9 yd. quadrilateral and 18 yd. for a 3 x 6 yd. quadrilateral.
B. Four possible perimeters are 40 yd. for a 2 x 18 yd. rectangle, 30 yd. for a 3 x 12 yd. rectangle, 26 yd. for a 4 x 9 yd. rectangle, and 24 yd. for a 6 x 6 yd. rectangle (a square is a rectangle).

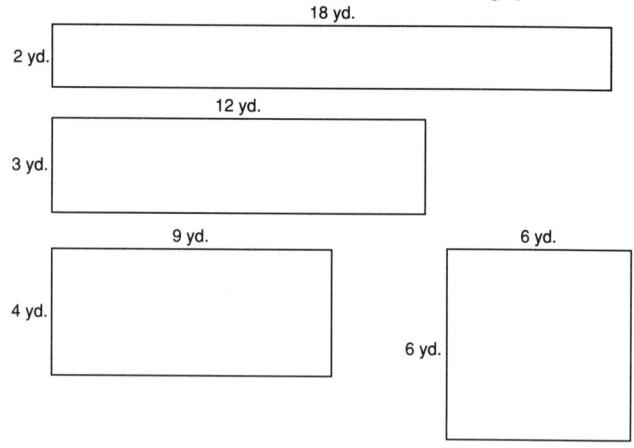

BRAINWORK: Drawings and perimeters will vary.

Page 58
Step 1: (3 in. x 40 yd.) x (3.5 in. x 40 yd.) = 16,800 yd.^{2}
Step 2: 2 ft. x 3 ft. = 6 ft.^{2} = 2 yd.^{2}; 16,800 yd.^{2} ÷ 2 yd.^{2} = 8,400 pieces of sod
Step 3: The position of students' shapes may vary. Football field = 1 in. x 3 in. rectangle ($^{40}/_{40}$ = 1 and $^{120}/_{40}$ = 3); announcer's booth = $^{1}/_{8}$ x $^{1}/_{4}$" rectangle ($^{15}/_{120}$ = $^{1}/_{8}$ and $^{30}/_{120}$ = $^{1}/_{4}$); bleachers = $^{1}/_{2}$ in. x 1$^{1}/_{2}$ in. rectangles, one on each side of the football field ($^{20}/_{40}$ = $^{1}/_{2}$ and $^{60}/_{40}$ = 1$^{1}/_{2}$)
Step 4: P = 2 (l + w) = 2 (40 yd. + 120 yd.) = 2 x 160 = 320 yd.
Step 5: 11 x 40 yd. = 440 yd.; 320 yd. + 440 yd. = 760 yd. x $0.23 = $174.80

BRAINWORK: field house = $^{1}/_{4}$ in. x $^{3}/_{4}$ in. ($^{10}/_{40}$ = $^{1}/_{4}$ and $^{30}/_{40}$ = $^{3}/_{4}$)

Page 59
1. 350 ft.³
2. 500 ft.³
3. 256 ft.³
4. 270 ft.³
5. 400 ft.³
6. Carton #2 holds the most. Carton #3 holds the least.

Predictions for the greatest and least volumes of the boxes in problems 7–12 may vary.

7. 216 cm³
8. 128 cm³
9. 160 cm³
10. 252 cm³
11. 120 cm³
12. 180 cm³

BRAINWORK: Drawings and answers will vary.

Page 60

	Circle	Measured Circumference	Diameter
1.	30 point	19 cm	6 cm
2.	40 point	16 cm	5 cm
3.	50 point	13 cm	4 cm
4.	60 point	9 cm	3 cm
5.	80 point	6 cm	2 cm
6.	bull's-eye	3 cm	1 cm

7. 3
8. 18.84 cm
9. 15.7 cm
10. 12.56 cm
11. 9.42 cm
12. 6.28 cm
13. 3.14 cm

BRAINWORK: Drawings and answers will vary.

Page 61
1. 3.14 in.²
2. 3.14 ft.²
3. 153.86 in.²
4. 9.62 ft.²
5. 113.04 cm²
6. 50.24 cm²
7. 1.77 cm²
8. 63.59 cm²
9. 19.63 in.²
10. 28.26 cm²
11. 38.47 cm²
12. 63.59 cm²

BRAINWORK:
1. 6.28 in.
2. 6.28 ft.
3. 43.96 in.
4. 10.99 ft.
5. 37.68 cm
6. 25.12 cm
7. 4.71 cm
8. 28.26 cm
9. 15.7 in.
10. 18.84 cm
11. 21.98 cm
12. 28.26 cm

Page 62
1. Red. Only 1 of the 7 candies is red.
2. Yellow. Four of the 7 candies are yellow.
3. No. There is a different number of each color of candy.
4. green: 2 in 7, blue: 0 in 7

Predictions and answers for the probability test may vary.

BRAINWORK: Predictions and answers may vary.

Page 63
Task 1: A. 1 in 4. Estimates may vary.
B. Answers will vary.
C. Answers will vary.

Task 2: A. 2 in 4 for the 2 squares that are the same color, 1 in 4 for the 2 squares that are different colors. Estimates may vary.
B. Answers will vary.
C. Answers will vary.

BRAINWORK: A. 3 in 4 for the 3 squares that are the same color, 1 in 4 for the 1 square that is a different color. Estimates may vary.
B. Answers will vary.
C. Answers will vary.

Page 64

Sum	Tiles with that sum	Number of tiles	Probability
0	0-0	1	¹⁄₂₈
1	0-1	1	¹⁄₂₈
2	1-1, 2-0	2	²⁄₂₈ = ¹⁄₁₄
3	1-2, 3-0	2	²⁄₂₈ = ¹⁄₁₄
4	1-3, 2-2, 4-0	3	³⁄₂₈
5	1-4, 2-3, 5-0	3	³⁄₂₈
6	1-5, 2-4, 3-3, 6-0	4	⁴⁄₂₈ = ¹⁄₇
7	1-6, 2-5, 3-4	3	³⁄₂₈
8	2-6, 3-5, 4-4	3	³⁄₂₈
9	3-6, 4-5	2	²⁄₂₈ = ¹⁄₁₄
10	4-6, 5-5	2	²⁄₂₈ = ¹⁄₁₄
11	5-6	1	¹⁄₂₈
12	6-6	1	¹⁄₂₈

1. ⁶⁄₂₈ = ³⁄₁₄ (3-6, 4-5, 4-6, 5-5, 5-6, 6-6)
2. ⁹⁄₂₈ (0-0, 0-1, 1-1, 2-0, 1-2, 3-0, 1-3, 2-2, 4-0)
3. ¹⁶⁄₂₈ = ⁴⁄₇ (0-0, 1-1, 2-0, 1-3, 2-2, 4-0, 1-5, 0-6, 2-4, 3-3, 2-6, 3-5, 4-4, 4-6, 5-5, 6-6)
4. ⁷⁄₂₈ = ¹⁄₄ (0-0, 1-1, 2-2, 3-3, 4-4, 5-5, 6-6)
5. ¹⁰⁄₂₈ = ⁵⁄₁₄ (0-0, 1-2, 3-0, 0-6, 1-5, 2-4, 3-3, 3-6, 4-5, 6-6)

BRAINWORK: There are 55 tiles in a set of double-9 dominoes. The chances of drawing the 0-0 tile are greater in the double-6 set (1 in 28, or ¹⁄₂₈). In the double-9 set, the odds are 1 in 55.

Page 66
Game 1 is fair. There are 3 even numbers that can be rolled (2, 4, and 6) and 3 odd numbers (1, 3, and 5). So there is a 3-in-6 chance of rolling either an even number or an odd number (³⁄₆ = ¹⁄₂, or a 50% chance).

Game 2 is not fair. There are 36 possible combinations that result from rolling 2 dice. Thirty of them result in pizza; only 6 result in hamburgers.

Game 3 is not fair. Only 12 of the 36 possible combinations result in playing cards, while 24 result in playing board games.

Game 4 is not fair. Only 7 of the 36 possible combinations result in sleeping inside, while 29 result in sleeping outside.

BRAINWORK: The rules for students' games will vary.

Page 67
1. mean = 331.6, median = 312, mode = 210, range = 395
2. mean = 144.3, median = 150, mode = 50, range = 290
3. mean = 19.3, median = 21, mode = 13, range = 19
4. mean = 3.9, median = 3, mode = 3, range = 7
5. mean = 711, median = 818, mode = 818, range = 2,075
6. mean = 47.9, median = 49, mode = 49, range = 4

BRAINWORK: Answers will vary.

Page 68
1. Stars: 65, Rangers: 50, Kings: 55, Red Wings: 36, Hawks: 40, Eagles: 60
2. Red Wings: 36, Hawks: 40, Rangers: 50, Kings: 55, Eagles: 60, Stars: 65
3. 306 goals
4. 51 goals
5. 5.42 goals
6. 29 goals
7. 24 goals
8. 15 goals; 16–24 goals

BRAINWORK: Predictions and answers will vary.

Page 70
1. a. 60 pounds   b. 35 pounds   c. 185 pounds
2. a. 550 pounds b. 700 pounds c. 350 pounds
3. Greenville; Mt. Trashmore
4. 30 pounds more
5. 165 pounds
6. b. soda pop
Garbageton; 905

BRAINWORK: 1,042.5 pounds

Page 71

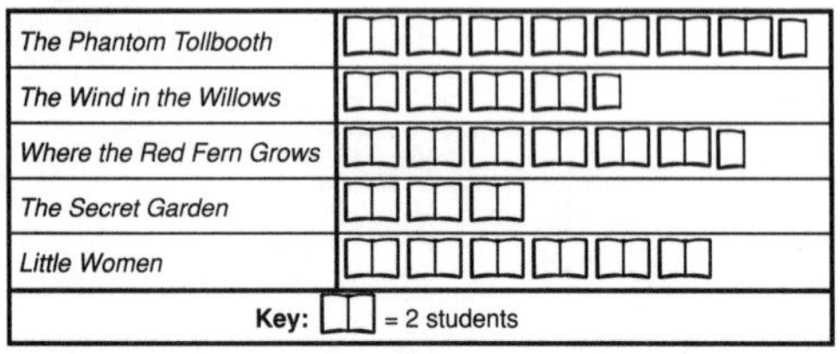

Book	Pictograph
The Phantom Tollbooth	
The Wind in the Willows	
Where the Red Fern Grows	
The Secret Garden	
Little Women	

Key: = 2 students

BRAINWORK: *The Phantom Tollbooth*: 60%; *The Wind in the Willows*: 36%; *Where the Red Fern Grows*: 52%; *The Secret Garden*: 24%; *Little Women*: 48%

Page 72
1. October: $65,000; April: $55,000; February: $50,000; December: $45,000
2. November: $10,000; January: $15,000; September: $15,000; May: $20,000
3. July and August
4. Answers will vary. Possible responses should note that the high months contain holidays that involve candy. For example, Halloween is in October; Easter is in April; Valentine's Day is in February; and Christmas, Hanukkah, and Kwanzaa are in December. The low months often follow the high months.
5. Answers will vary.
6. $405,000

BRAINWORK: $33,750

Page 73

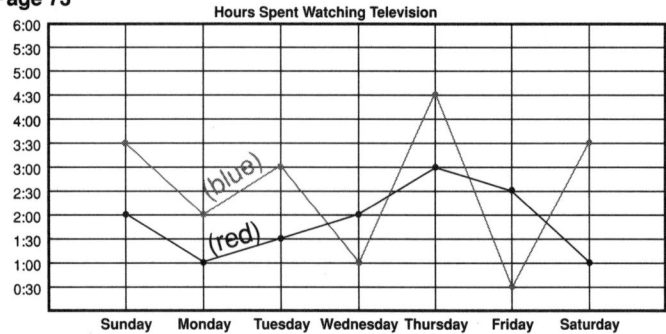

Hours Spent Watching Television (line graph: blue and red lines, Sunday–Saturday, 0:30 to 6:00)

BRAINWORK: Graphs will vary.

Page 74
1. vanilla
2. 43%
3. 29%
4. mint chocolate chip and peanut butter cup
5. mint chocolate chip: 10; orange-pineapple and peach: 9; vanilla: 25
6. peanut butter cup: $30.00; fudge brownie: $15.00; top 3 flavors: $180.00
7. $265.00
8. Answers will vary.
9. Answers will vary.

BRAINWORK: The circle graph should show the following information: $50.00 on vanilla, $36.00 on chocolate, $34.00 on strawberry, $20.00 on mint chocolate chip, $20.00 on peanut butter cup, $14.00 on orange-pineapple, $10.00 on fudge brownie, $6.00 on cookies 'n' cream, $6.00 on black cherry, and $4.00 on peach.

Page 75
1. Jokes Preferred by Adult Female Hyenas — knock-knock jokes 1/2, elephant jokes 1/4, puns 1/8, waiter jokes 1/8
2. Jokes Preferred by Adult Male Hyenas — waiter jokes 50, knock-knock jokes 20, elephant jokes 10, puns 20
3. Jokes Preferred by Young Hyenas — elephant jokes 3/10, knock-knock jokes 1/5, didn't understand the jokes 1/10, waiter jokes 1/5, puns 1/5

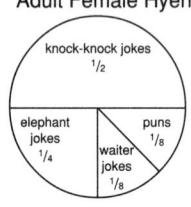

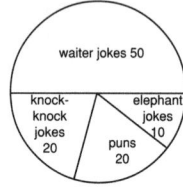

BRAINWORK: Answers will vary.

110

Page 76
1. 42 years old
2. 10 presidents
3. 27 years
4. 18 presidents
5. 51 years old
6. 0 presidents
7. 54.6 years old

BRAINWORK: Graphs will vary. Below is one possible bar graph. (Bar graph: Number of Presidents vs Age — 40s: 3, 50s: 10, 60s: 5)

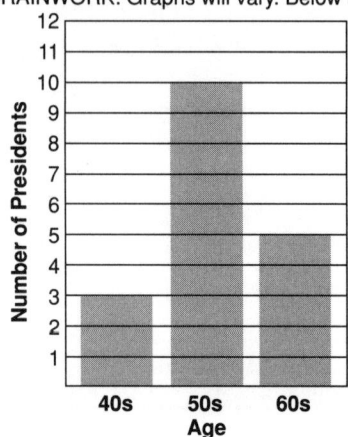

Page 77
Part I:
Title: **Heights of Petersville Little League Players**

Stems	Leaves
4	8 9
5	2 2 4 5 5 6 7 7 8 8 9
6	0 1 1 1 2 3

Part II:
1. 57
2. 61
3. 48, 63
4. 15 inches
5. 4, 5
6. large

BRAINWORK: 48 inches = 4 feet tall; 63 inches = 5 feet 3 inches tall

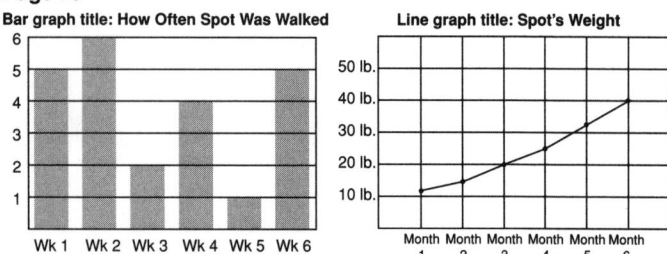

Page 78
Bar graph title: How Often Spot Was Walked
Line graph title: Spot's Weight
Pictograph title: Spot's Behavior 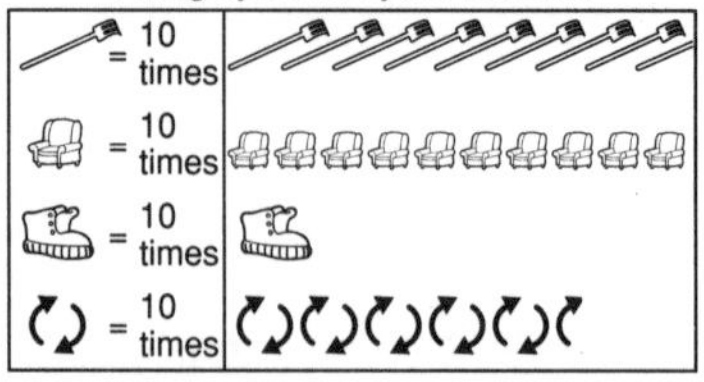
Circle graph title: $300.00 Spent on Spot — Toys $25.00, Medical $50.00, Food $50.00, Replacing Shoes $75.00, Bedding/Supplies $100.00

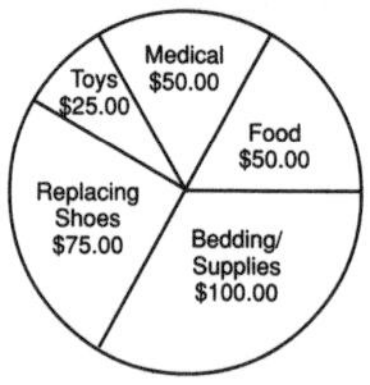

BRAINWORK: The circle graph is the only graph that should be used to display the money table. A circle graph shows parts of a whole. The other 3 graphs are interchangeable because their data is basically the same.

Page 79
1. 2:10 P.M.
2. 33 miles
3. Roberta—12; Rex—9; Rhonda—11; Ray—11; Rufus—14
4. 1:35 P.M.
5. $70.05

BRAINWORK: Answers will vary.

Page 80
1. Zach, 12 pounds
2. Pablo, 20 pounds
3. Bertha, 24 ounces
4. Opie, 30 ounces
5. Mora, 10 pounds

BRAINWORK: Drawings will vary.

Page 81

Student A	Student B	Student C
1st per.—technology	1st per.—math	1st per.—English
2nd per.—social studies	2nd per.—social studies	2nd per.—science
3rd per.—math	3rd per.—science	3rd per.—technology
4th per.—English	4th per.—English	4th per.—social studies
5th per.—science	5th per.—technology	5th per.—math

BRAINWORK: Student A—Rob; Student B—Rick; Student C—Renee

Page 82

Mary Lou—Wednesday, 9:00 A.M., Lady
Billy—Monday, 11:00 A.M., Rex
Chuck—Tuesday, 10:00 A.M., Charlie
Dottie—Thursday, 1:00 P.M., Gus

BRAINWORK: Answers will vary.

Page 83

1. 83
2. 75
3. 49
4. 282
5. 357
6. 262
7. 222
8. 333
9. 335
10. 701

BRAINWORK: Solutions may vary. Here is one solution:
3
4–5–6
7

Page 84

Answers may vary. One possible solution:
Angry Alice—3 large muffins, 3 small muffins
Frustrated Frank—2 large muffins, 0 small muffins
Sour Sam—2 large muffins, 5 small muffins
Irritable Irene—0 large muffins, 1 small muffin
Raging Roger—4 large muffins, 2 small muffins
11; 11

BRAINWORK: Answers will vary.

Page 85

1. bch, tr
   bch, pln
   bch, car
   mtns, tr
   mtns, pln
   mtns, car
   theme pk, tr
   theme pk, pln
   theme pk, car

2. Q D N
    2 0 1
    1 3 0
    1 2 2
    1 1 4
    1 0 6
    0 5 1
    0 4 3
    0 3 5
    0 2 7
    0 1 9
    0 0 11

3. thick, pepp, reg ch
   thick, pepp, x ch
   thick, saus, reg ch
   thick, saus, x ch
   thick, mshrm, reg ch
   thick, mshrm, x ch
   thick, no top, reg ch
   thick, no top, x ch
   thin, pepp, reg ch
   thin, pepp, x ch
   thin, saus, reg ch
   thin, saus, x ch
   thin, mush, reg ch
   thin, mush, x ch
   thin, no top, reg ch
   thin, no top, x ch

4. bro, ph, T-sh
   bro, ph, bsb cp
   bro, ph, kychn
   bro, pstcd, T-sh
   bro, pstcd, bsb cp
   bro, pstcd, kychn
   bro, eml, T-sh
   bro, eml, bsb cp
   bro, eml, kychn
   sis, phn, T-sh
   sis, phn, bsb cp
   sis, phn, kychn
   sis, pstcd, T-sh
   sis, pstcd, bsb cp
   sis, pstcd, kychn
   sis, eml, T-sh
   sis, eml, bsb cp
   sis, eml, kychn

BRAINWORK: Likely; 12/16 or 3/4

Page 86

1. **hat**
   star
   star
   star
   lightning bolt
   lightning bolt
   lightning bolt
   crystal ball
   crystal ball
   crystal ball
   robe
   star
   lightning bolt
   crystal ball
   star
   lightning bolt
   crystal ball
   star
   lightning bolt
   crystal ball

2. high, red, fast
   high, red, med
   high, red, slow
   high, black, fast
   high, black, med
   high, black, slow
   high, plaid, fast
   high, plaid, med
   high, plaid, slow
   low, red, fast
   low, red, med
   low, red, slow
   low, black, fast
   low, black, med
   low, black, slow
   low, plaid, fast
   low, plaid, med
   low, plaid, slow
   4 cpts; 12 cpts; 2 cpts

3. mnbm, gld, blk
   mnbm, gld, prpl
   mnbm, gld, rd
   mnbm, cpr, blk
   mnbm, cpr, prpl
   mnbm, cpr, rd
   mnbm, wd, blk
   mnbm, wd, prpl
   mnbm, wd, rd
   stdst, gld, blk
   stdst, gld, prpl
   stdst, gld, rd
   stdst, cpr, blk
   stdst, cpr, prpl
   stdst, cpr, rd
   stdst, wd, blk
   stdst, wd, prpl
   stdst, wd, rd

4 outfits

$25.00—Any kit that includes a gold wand handle and a black or red cape.
$10.00—Any kit that includes a purple cape and a copper or a wood wand handle.

BRAINWORK: Answers may vary but should fall between the range of $14.00 to $20.00. Accept reasonable explanations based on given information.

Page 87

Player	Assists	Goals	Attempts
11	13	6	19
8	10	6	25
24	24	12	31
15	9	24	24
1	20	12	20
12	18	9	32

1. #24, #15, #12
2. 69 goals
3. 25 more assists
4. 82 more attempts

BRAINWORK: Answers will vary but should include the 3 players they think should go to the all-star game and why.

Page 88

1.

Day	Mon.	Tues.	Wed.	Thurs.	Fri.	Sat.	Sun.
Gum	3	6	9	12	15	18	21

Jordan will chew 21 pieces of gum.

2.

Day	1	2	3	4	5	6	7	8	9	10	11	12	13	14	15	16	17	18	19	20	21
Lemon	x		x		x		x		x		x		x		x		x		x		x
Tangerine		x			x			x			x			x			x			x	

She will chew both types of gum 3 times.

3.

Person	1	5	10	15	20	25	30
Gumball	x	x	x	x	x	x	x
Stick		x		x		x	
Sucker		x			x		x

Five people received a gumball and a sucker. Two people received all 3.

4.

Leonard	6	12	18	24	30	36	42
Cindy	8	16	24	32	40	48	56

Leonard will blow 42 bubbles.

BRAINWORK:

Person	31	35	40	45	50	55	60
Gumball		x	x	x	x	x	x
Stick	x		x		x		x
Sucker		x		x		x	

Ten people would receive a gumball and a sucker. Five people would receive all 3.

Page 89

1. Answer: 20 sticks; Pattern: multiply by 2
2. Answer: 10 jars; Pattern: divide by 5
3. Answer: 90 pizzas; Pattern: subtract 15, add 10
4. Answer: 7 onions, 1 pepper; Pattern: subtract 1 onion and 1 pepper
5. 16 slices, 8 pieces, 8 drinks; 200 slices, 100 pieces, 100 drinks; 400 slices, 200 pieces, 200 drinks

BRAINWORK: 8 packs, 16 packs, 23 packs

Page 90

A. 1, 3, 5, <u>7</u>, 9, <u>11</u>, <u>13</u>, 15, 17, 19, <u>21</u>
B. 2, 4, 6, 8, <u>10</u>, <u>12</u>, 14, <u>16</u>, <u>18</u>, <u>20</u>, 22
C. 15, <u>20</u>, 25, 30, <u>35</u>, <u>40</u>, 45, <u>50</u>, <u>55</u>
D. 1, 3, 9, <u>27</u>, 81, <u>243</u>, 729, <u>2,187</u>, 6,561
E. 1, 2, 3, 5, 7, 11, <u>13</u>, 17, <u>19</u>, 23, 29, <u>31</u>
F. 4, 8, 12, <u>16</u>, 20, <u>24</u>, 28, 32, 36, <u>40</u>, <u>44</u>
G. 2, 8, 6, 12, 10, <u>16</u>, 14, 20, <u>18</u>, <u>24</u>, 22
H. 7, 9, 8, 10, 9, <u>11</u>, <u>10</u>, 12, 11, <u>13</u>, <u>12</u>, 14, 13
I. 10, 7, <u>12</u>, 9, 14, 11, <u>16</u>, <u>13</u>, 18, 15, <u>20</u>, 17, <u>22</u>, 19
J. 4, 8, 9, 18, <u>19</u>, <u>38</u>, 39, <u>78</u>, <u>79</u>, 158, 159, <u>318</u>

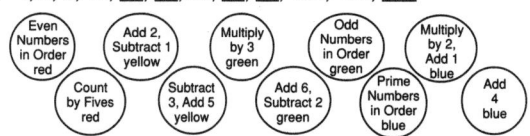

Even Numbers in Order – red
Add 2, Subtract 1 – yellow
Multiply by 3 – green
Odd Numbers in Order – green
Multiply by 2, Add 1 – blue
Count by Fives – red
Subtract 3, Add 5 – yellow
Add 6, Subtract 2 – green
Prime Numbers in Order – blue
Add 4 – blue

BRAINWORK: Students' patterns will vary. Accept all reasonable patterns.

Page 91

1. 2nd seat
2. salmon
3. marlin
4. 3 eels
5. 27 fish
6. thresher shark

BRAINWORK: Answers will vary but should incorporate the act-it-out strategy. Accept all reasonable problems.

Page 92

1. Solutions may vary. One possible solution for each is shown.

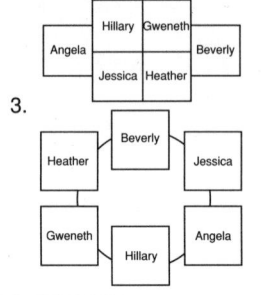

	Hillary	Gweneth	
Angela			Beverly
	Jessica	Heather	

2.

Angela	Heather	Jessica
Beverly	Hillary	Gweneth

3.

```
      Beverly
Heather        Jessica
Gweneth        Angela
      Hillary
```

4.

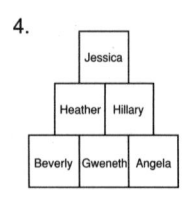

```
        Jessica
    Heather  Hillary
Beverly  Gweneth  Angela
```

BRAINWORK:

Hillary	Angela	Heather	Gweneth	Beverly	Jessica
last					first

Page 93

1. Answers may vary slightly.
   Bill, Pat, Kim, Jan, Jack, Sue, Lee, Sam (around circle)

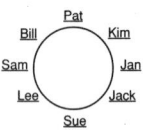

2. 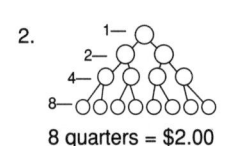 8 quarters = $2.00

3. Bow, Bow, Bow, Bow, Bow, Bow, Bow, Bow, Bow, Bow / Paper, Paper, Paper, Paper, Paper, Paper, Paper, Paper
   Five presents have pink bows and pink wrapping paper.

4. 45 minutes to play the game

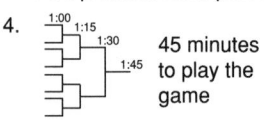

5. red 3, 4, black 1; 3 wore red only

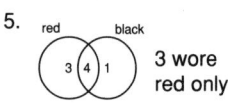

BRAINWORK: Drawings may vary.

Page 94

Drawings will vary. Possible drawings are shown below.

1. 1,100 feet (200 feet)
2. 540 feet (60 feet sides)
3. 300 feet, 600 feet (100 feet, 50 feet)
4. 6,400 feet (2000 feet, 800 feet)
5. 35 miles (15 miles, 60 miles, 20 miles)

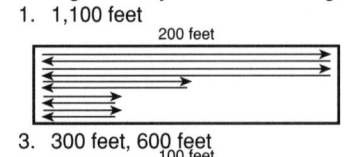

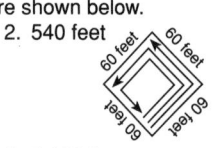

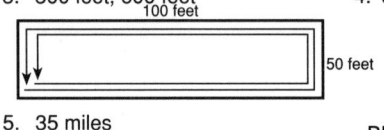

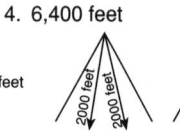

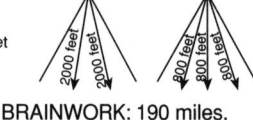

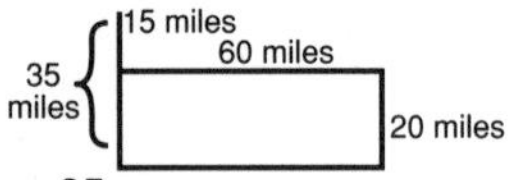

BRAINWORK: 190 miles, Robin rides the farthest, 130 miles

Page 95

A. yellow (associative)
B. green (distributive)
C. blue (commutative)
D. red (identity)
E. yellow (associative)
F. green (distributive)
G. blue (commutative)
H. yellow (associative)
I. red (identity)
J. blue (commutative)

BRAINWORK: Answers may vary. Possible answers include
(7 × 3) + (7 × 3) = 42; (13 × 10) + (13 × 2) = 156; (3 × 7) + (3 × 2) = 27.

Page 96

1. 27 + 26 + 24 + n = 98
   n = 21
   21 years old
2. 16n = 56
   n = 3.5
   3.5 minutes
3. n + 2n = 36
   n = 12
   24 hours; 12 hours
4. 4n = $245,624.00
   n = $61,406.00
   $61,406.00
5. n + (n + 1) + (n + 2) = 18
   n = 5
   5 hours; 6 hours; 7 hours
6. n + n + $10,000.00 = $30,000.00
   n = $10,000.00
   $20,000.00; $10,000.00

BRAINWORK: 25,000 + 75,000 + 2n + n = 460,000; n = 120,000 CDs;
The group sold 240,000 CDs on the 3rd day.

Page 97

Answers may vary slightly.
1. Input: 8; Output: 56, 4
   Rule: Multiply by 8.
2. Input: 16; Output: 15, 14
   Rule: Divide by 4.
3. Input: 66; Output: 5, 17
   Rule: Divide by 3.
4. Input: 10; Output: 81, 31
   Rule: Multiply by 2; then add 1.
5. Input: 5, 0; Output: 36
   Rule: Square the number (multiply by itself).
6. Input: 18; Output: 90, 48, 400
   Rule: Multiply by 2.
7. Input: 125, 115; Output: 11, 17
   Rule: Multiply by 5.
8. Input: 9, 15; Output: 72
   Rule: Multiply by 10; then add 2.

BRAINWORK: Answers will vary.

Page 98

Grade 3: x + 2

x Books Read	0	1	2	3	4	5
y Prizes Earned	2	3	4	5	6	7

Grade 4: x − 3

x Books Read	3	4	5	6	7	8
y Prizes Earned	0	1	2	3	4	5

Grade 5: ½ x

x Books Read	2	4	6	8	10	12
y Prizes Earned	1	2	3	4	5	6

Grade 6: 3x

x Books Read	0	1	2	3	4	5
y Prizes Earned	0	3	6	9	12	15

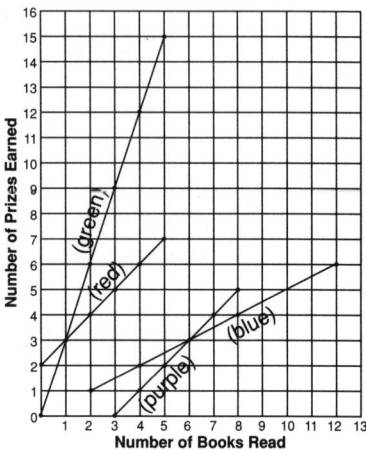

(Graph showing lines: green, red, blue, purple — Number of Prizes Earned vs Number of Books Read)

Page 99

x	y
−2	2
−2	1
−2	0
−2	−1
−2	−2

x	y
−2	−2
−1	−2
0	−2
1	−2
2	−2

x	y
2	−2
2	−1
2	0
2	1
2	2

x	y
2	2
1	2
0	2
−1	2
−2	2

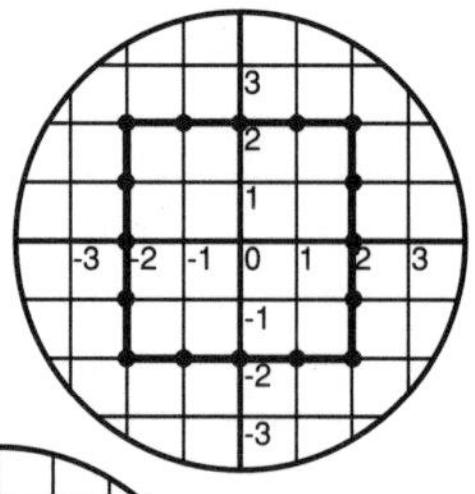

(x, y)	(x, y)	(x, y)	(x, y)
(0, 3)	(−3, 0)	(0, −3)	(3, 0)
(−1, 2)	(−2, −1)	(1, −2)	(2, 1)
(−2, 1)	(−1, −2)	(2, −1)	(1, 2)
(−3, 0)	(0, −3)	(3, 0)	(0, 3)

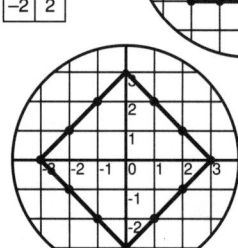

Page 100

The following numbers or equations should be crossed out:
1. 5,454 or 5,544; 4,554
2. 147,714 or 147,147; 171,474
3. 6.003; 0.06
4. 4/8, 3/5
5. (3 + 8); (16 ÷ 4)
6. 1/2; .44

BRAINWORK: Answers will vary.

Page 101

1. f = 33
2. o = 5
3. k = 818
4. s = 103
5. e = 273
6. r = 4
7. l = 10
8. n = 252
9. a = 190
10. c = 6

BRAINWORK: cornflakes

Page 102

Mt. Peak: 6 miles; **Mt. Grande:** 14 miles, 4 miles; **Mt. High Point:** 17 miles; **Mt. Low:** 9 miles

Clue 2: up Mt. Steep; x = 2(3); x = 6
Clue 3: down Mt. Grande; 4 + 6 = x + 6; x = 4
Clue 4: down Mt. High Point; 6 + 11 = x; x = 17
Clue 5: down Mt. Low; 8 + x = 17; x = 9
Clue 6: up Mt. Grande; x + 3 + 4 + 6 + 11 + 4 + 6 + 17 + 8 + 9 = 82;
          x + 68 = 82; x = 14

BRAINWORK: Melinda traveled 1.5 miles per hour.
(123 hours ÷ 82 miles = 1.5 miles per hour)

Page 103

1. −10°C
2. 3°C
3. −20°C
4. −13°C
5. 29°C
6. −1°C
7. −2°C
8. −4°C; 11°C
9. 0°C
10. −7°C

BRAINWORK: Pictures will vary. The thermometer should show a temperature of 0°C or less.